ALFRED'S

PIANO 101

AN EXCITING GROUP COURSE FOR ADULTS
WHO WANT TO PLAY PIANO FOR FUN!

E. L. LANCASTER / KENON D. RENFROW

W9-BXN-268

Foreword

Piano 101, Book 1, is a group course designed for adults with little or no keyboard experience who want to study piano for fun. Its easy-to-use format also is effective in private lessons. Specifically, it can be used for college piano classes of non-music majors, continuing education classes and music dealer in-store programs.

Piano 101 is easy to use. It contains 15 units. In college classes for non-music majors, each unit is designed to be covered in one week, thus filling an entire semester of study. However, teachers who are using the book in college classes or other situations should move at a pace appropriate for each individual class. The title page of each unit contains the objectives for the unit, a space to record assignments and a section called *"Did You Know?"* This section briefly discusses elements of music history or music theory of general interest to piano students. It can serve as a spring board for further class discussion. Major headings (including all new concepts) are identified by a check mark (✓). Measures are numbered in all examples to promote ease of use in the classroom.

The reading approach is eclectic, combining the best elements of intervallic and multi-key reading. Reading exercises are designed to promote movement over the entire keyboard while maintaining the advantages of playing in familiar positions. Reading examples are a mixture of familiar music and newly composed pieces.

Suggestions for counting are given but the approach used is left to the discretion of the teacher. Rhythms and note values are introduced systematically and specially designed rhythm reading exercises promote rhythmic security.

The student begins to play music immediately. Repertoire has been carefully chosen to appeal to adults who are playing the piano for fun and includes tasteful arrangements of familiar music. A section of supplementary repertoire begins on page 138 for those students who need additional music or for teachers who like a wider choice of music for students. The supplementary repertoire was chosen to represent a variety of levels and can be used throughout the book.

Each unit contains a balance of new information with materials that reinforce concepts presented in previous units. Written review worksheets appear periodically throughout the text.

Theory, technique, sight-reading, repertoire, harmonization from lead sheets, ear training and ensemble activities are taught thoroughly and consistently throughout the text. The emphasis on ear training and harmonizing melodies from lead sheets will be helpful to those students who are interested in playing by ear. Teacher's examples for all ear training examples are contained in Appendix A (page 153).

Technique is developed in a systematic way throughout the entire book. Repertoire, lead sheet melodies, technical exercises and sight-reading examples are carefully fingered to aid the student in developing good technique.

This book is fully supported by Compact Discs (CD) and General MIDI (GM) disks. Each example in the text that contains an accompaniment is identified by an icon that shows the disk number and TRACK number for the example: ◀») **1-1(43).** The first number after the icon denotes the CD/GM disk number. The second number is the TRACK number on the CD and the Type 0 MIDI file on the GM disk. The third number (in parentheses) is the TRACK number of the Type 1 MIDI file on the GM disk. (See MIDI disk documentation for more information on MIDI file types.) Accompaniments range from simple drum patterns to full orchestrations. These accompaniments add musical interest and motivate students to complete assignments both in the classroom and in the practice room.

A Teacher's Handbook for the text serves as an aid in curriculum development and daily lesson planning. The Handbook contains suggested daily lesson plans, suggested assignments following each lesson plan, teaching tips for each unit, suggested examinations for the semester and answer keys for the written exercises and review worksheets. It also suggests ways to successfully integrate keyboard and computer technology into the curriculum.

Upon completion of this book, students will have a strong grasp of keyboard skills, piano repertoire and musical styles, and will be ready to begin *Piano 101, Book 2.*

Thanks to David B. Smith for suggesting the title of the book.

Table of Contents

P I A N O 1 0 1 , B O O K 1

Playing on Black Keys

Objectives

Upon completion of this unit the student will be able to:

1. Use correct posture and hand position at the keyboard.

2. Identify fingers by number.

3. Apply basic rhythmic concepts to performance at the keyboard.

4. Perform melodies on two- and three-black-key groups.

Assignments

Week of _____

Write your assignments for the week in the space below.

_____

_____

_____

_____

_____

_____

_____

_____

_____

_____

_____

_____

_____

_____

Did You Know?

The Power of Music

Congratulations on your decision to study piano. Most experts agree that the piano is the most essential of all musical instruments. It is the best audio-visual aid to learning music in general, and there can be much joy in the process as well. Music, like nothing else known to man, is a universal language of human emotion. It has the power to evoke many moods and emotions, and transcends barriers of culture, language, social status and education. Some of the earliest writings refer to music and its importance. Socrates said, "Let me control the music of a nation, and I care not who makes its laws." Plato wrote that the type of music to which one listens has a tremendous effect on what type of person one becomes. Consider the power of music as you begin your quest to learn through the medium of piano!

How to Sit at the Keyboard

Sit tall! Leaning slightly forward, let your arms hang loosely from the shoulders with your elbows slightly higher than the keys. The bench must face the piano squarely. Position your knees slightly under the keyboard, with your feet flat on the floor. The right foot may be slightly forward.

Hand Position

Curve your fingers when you play, as though you have a bubble in your hand.

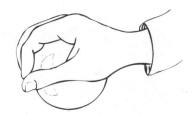

Curved fingers bring the thumb into the proper playing position and provide an arch that allows the thumb to pass under the fingers or the fingers to cross over the thumb.

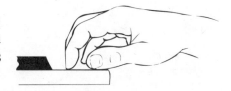

Finger Numbers

The fingers of the left hand (LH) and the right hand (RH) are numbered as shown. The thumb is the first finger of each hand.

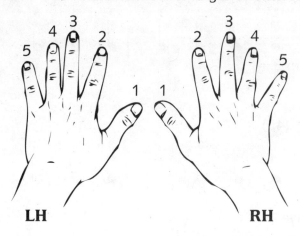

LH   RH

Basic Note Values

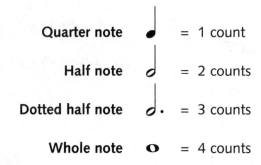

Quarter note	♩	= 1 count
Half note	♪	= 2 counts
Dotted half note	♩.	= 3 counts
Whole note	o	= 4 counts

Clap (or tap) the following rhythm. Clap once for each note, counting aloud. Notice how the bar lines divide the music into measures of equal duration.

Compact Discs and General MIDI Disks*

◀))) **1-1 (43)** ➤ Track number of Type 1 file on GM disk

Track number on CD or Type 0 file on GM disk

CD / GM Disk Number

◀))) **1-1 (43)**

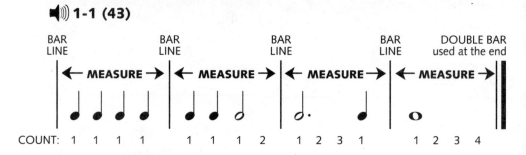

BAR LINE	BAR LINE	BAR LINE	BAR LINE	DOUBLE BAR used at the end

← MEASURE → | ← MEASURE → | ← MEASURE → | ← MEASURE →

COUNT: 1 1 1 1   1 1 1 2   1 2 3 1   1 2 3 4

RHYTHM READING

Tap the following rhythms on a desk or tabletop, with the indicated hands and finger numbers.

Hands separately:

◀))) **1-2 (44)**

Fingers: 1   1   2   2   3   4   5   5   5   4   4   3   2   1

1. RH

COUNT: 1   1   1   1   1   1   1   2   1   1   1   1   1   1   1   2

◀))) **1-3 (45)**

1   2   3   3   4   5   5   4   3   3   3   2   1

2. RH

*See page 2.

1-4 (46)

3. LH
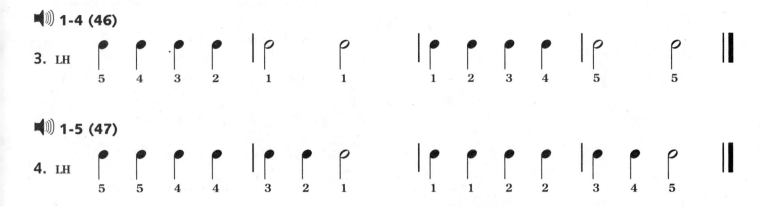

5 4 3 2 1 1 1 2 3 4 5 5

 1-5 (47)

4. LH
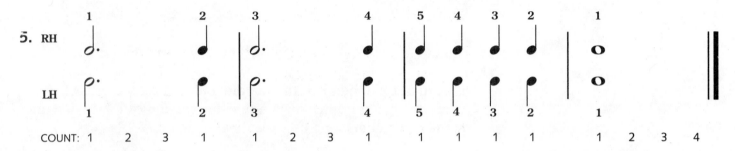

5 5 4 4 3 2 1 1 1 2 2 3 4 5

Hands together:

 1-6 (48)

5. RH / LH
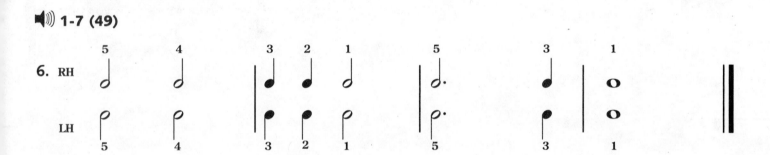

COUNT: 1 2 3 1 1 2 3 1 1 1 1 1 1 2 3 4

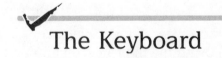 **1-7 (49)**

6. RH / LH

The Keyboard

The keyboard is made up of white keys and black keys. The black keys are in groups of twos and threes. On the keyboard, down is to the left, and up is to the right. As you move left, the tones sound lower. As you move right, the tones sound higher.

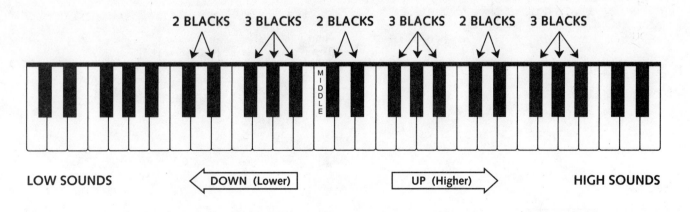

2 BLACKS   3 BLACKS   2 BLACKS   3 BLACKS   2 BLACKS   3 BLACKS

LOW SOUNDS   ← DOWN (Lower)   UP (Higher) →   HIGH SOUNDS

Two-Black-Key Groups

LH

1. Using LH 2 3, begin at the middle and play all the 2-black-key groups going down the keyboard (both keys at once).

RH

2. Using RH 2 3, begin at the middle and play all the 2-black-key groups going up the keyboard (both keys at once).

3. With RH 2 3, begin at the middle and play all the 2-black-key groups going up the keyboard, using the indicated rhythm and finger numbers (one key at a time).

1-8 (50)

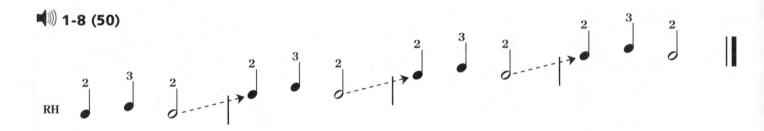

4. With LH 2 3, begin at the middle and play all the 2-black-key groups going down the keyboard, using the indicated rhythm and finger numbers (one key at a time).

1-9 (51)

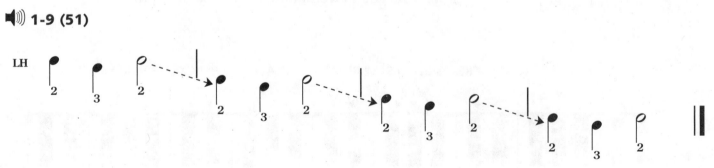

Three-Black Key Groups

1. Using LH 2 3 4, begin at the middle and play all the 3-black-key groups going down the keyboard (all 3 keys at once).

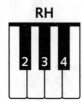

2. Using RH 2 3 4, begin at the middle and play all the 3-black-key groups going up the keyboard (all 3 keys at once).

3. With RH 2 3 4, begin at the middle and play all the 3-black-key groups going up the keyboard, using the indicated rhythm and finger numbers (one key at a time).

🔊 1-10 (52)

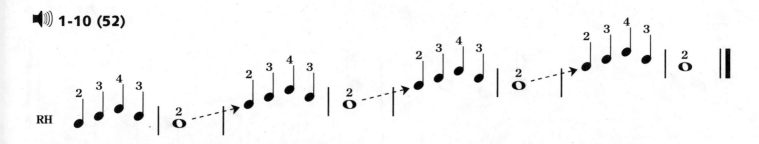

4. With LH 2 3 4, begin at the middle and play all the 3-black-key groups going down the keyboard, using the indicated rhythm and finger numbers (one key at a time).

🔊 1-11 (53)

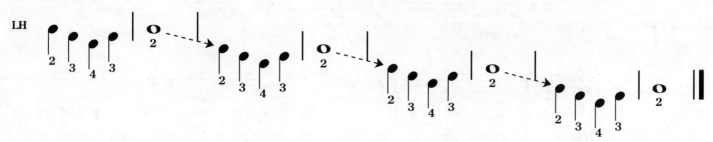

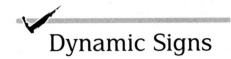

Dynamic Signs

Dynamic signs tell how loudly or softly to play.
Common dynamic signs include:

mf *(mezzo forte)* = moderately loud

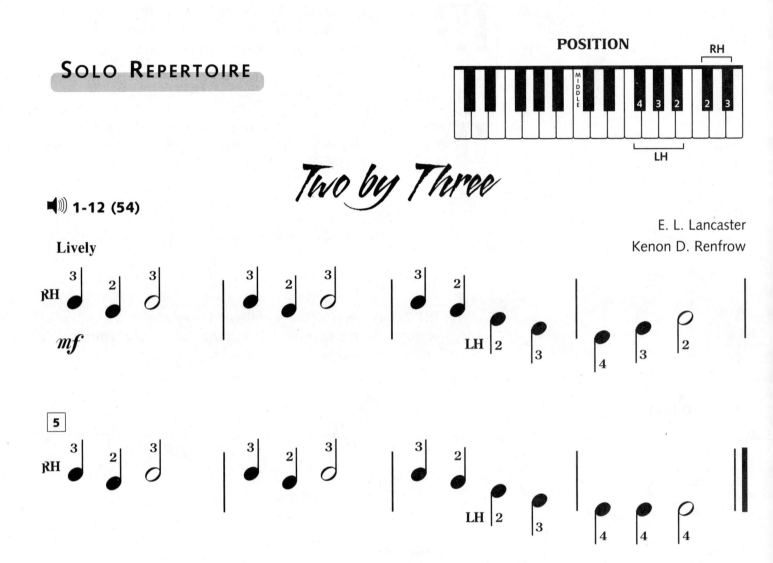

Two by Three

🔊 1-12 (54)

E. L. Lancaster
Kenon D. Renfrow

TEACHER ACCOMPANIMENT*

*Note: All accompaniments are for a second piano unless otherwise noted.

Playing on White Keys

UNIT TWO

Objectives

Upon completion of this unit the student will be able to:

1. Name, find and play all white keys on the keyboard.
2. Perform simple melodies on white keys.
3. Identify rests and apply them to performance at the keyboard.
4. Tap two-part rhythm patterns.
5. Aurally distinguish low from high sounds, sounds that move up or down and simple rhythm patterns.

Assignments

Week of _____

Write your assignments for the week in the space below.

_____

_____

_____

_____

_____

_____

_____

_____

_____

_____

_____

_____

_____

Did You Know?

History of the Piano

Although the piano was invented in 1709 by Bartolommeo Cristofori in Florence, Italy, piano music and the piano as we know it today did not really come into its own until much later in the 18th century. Before this time, the harpsichord and clavichord were the instruments of choice. Cristofori's instrument, called the pianoforte, allowed the performer to play both soft and loud depending on touch. This allowed for a greater degree of expression. The pianoforte was the direct forerunner of the acoustic piano that we know today.

Naming White Keys

Piano keys are named for the first seven letters of the alphabet. The key names are A B C D E F G, used over and over! The lowest key on the piano is A. The C nearest the middle of the piano is called middle C. The highest key on the piano is C. Going up the keyboard, the notes sound higher and higher. While most acoustic pianos have 88 keys, some digital keyboards may have fewer.

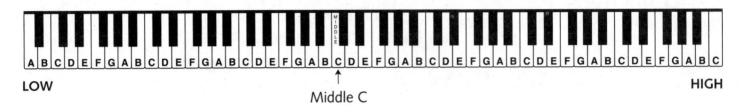

LOW

Middle C

HIGH

Beginning at the low end and moving *up* the keyboard, play and name every white key beginning with the bottom **A,** using the indicated rhythm. Use LH 3 for keys below the middle of the keyboard. Use RH 3 for keys above the middle of the keyboard.

◀))) **1-13 (55)**

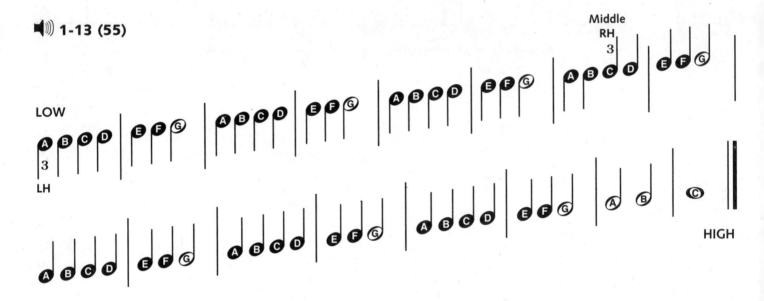

Play all the **A**'s on your piano.

Beginning at the low end and moving *up* the keyboard, play every **A,** using ♩♩♩ on each key. Say the name of each key aloud as you play. Use LH 3 for keys below middle C on the keyboard. Use RH 3 for middle C and keys above middle C on the keyboard. Repeat this exercise for **B, C, D, E, F** and **G.**

Play all the **B**'s.

Play all the **C**'s.

Play all the **D**'s.

Play all the **E**'s.

Play all the **F**'s.

Play all the **G**'s.

Octave

An **octave** is the distance from one key on the keyboard to the next key (lower or higher) with the same letter name.

C-D-E Groups

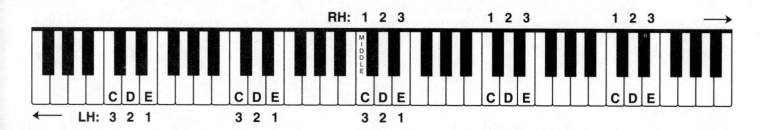

With RH 1 2 3, begin on middle **C** and play all of the **C-D-E** groups going *up* the keyboard, using the indicated rhythm and finger numbers.

🔊 **1-14 (56)**

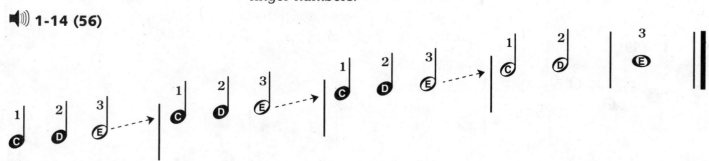

With LH 1 2 3, begin on the **E** above middle **C** and play all of the **E-D-C** groups going *down* the keyboard, using the indicated rhythm and finger numbers.

🔊 **1-15 (57)**

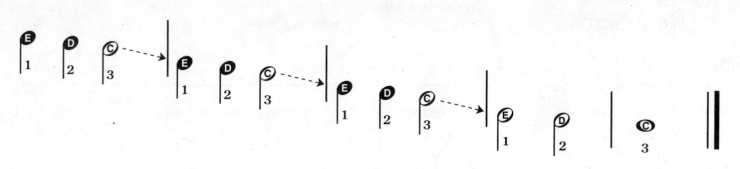

F-G-A-B Groups

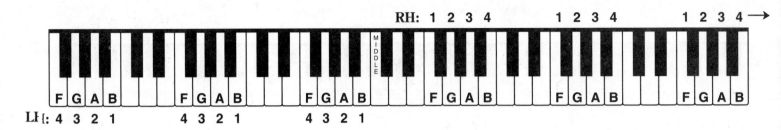

With RH 1 2 3 4, begin on the **F** above middle **C** and play all of the **F-G-A-B** groups going *up* the keyboard using the indicated rhythm and finger numbers.

🔊 **1-16 (58)**

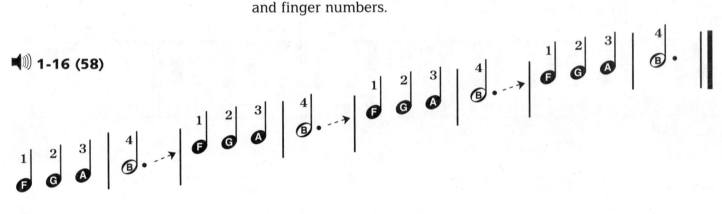

With LH 1 2 3 4, begin on the **B** below middle **C** and play all of the **B-A-G-F** groups going *down* the keyboard using the indicated rhythm and finger numbers.

🔊 **1-17 (59)**

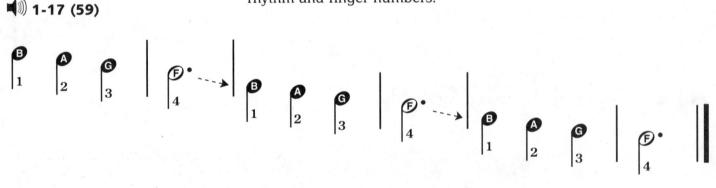

✓ New Signs

Dynamic signs

p (piano) = soft
f (forte) = loud

First ending (⌐1.⎤): play first time only.

Second ending (⌐2.⎤): play second time only.

Repeat sign (:‖): repeat from the beginning.

starting key: **RH**

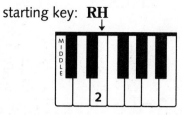

Summer Night

🔊 **1-18 (60)**

Kenon D. Renfrow

Flowing

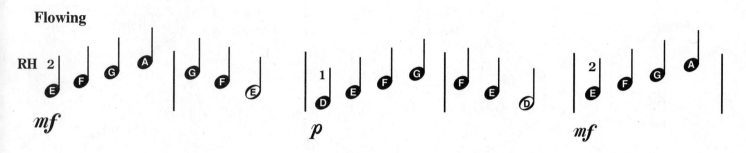

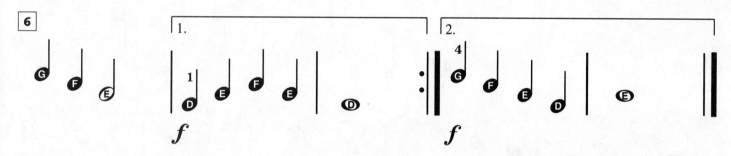

OPTIONAL : Play *Summer Night* with the LH beginning with finger 4.

TEACHER ACCOMPANIMENT

Rests

Rests are signs for silence.

Quarter rest (𝄽) means rest for the value of a quarter note.
Half rest (▬) means rest for the value of a half note.
Whole rest (▬) means rest for the value of a whole note or any whole measure.

 SOLO REPERTOIRE

 *Simple Elegance*

starting key: **LH**

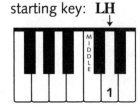

🔊 **1-19 (61)**

Moderate

Kenon D. Renfrow

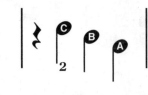

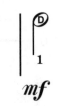

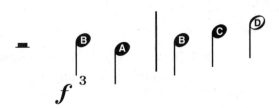

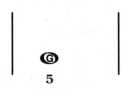

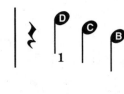

OPTIONAL: Play *Simple Elegance* with the RH beginning with finger 5.

TEACHER ACCOMPANIMENT

Moderate (♩ = 180)

detached

RHYTHM READING

Tap the following rhythm patterns using RH for notes with stems going up and LH for notes with stems going down. Tap hands separately first, and then hands together, always counting aloud.

🔊 1-20 (62)

1.

🔊 1-21 (63)

2.

🔊 1-22 (64)

3.

🔊 1-23 (65)

4.

EAR TRAINING

1. Your teacher will play LOW or HIGH sounds.
   • Circle LOW if you hear LOW sounds.
   • Circle HIGH if you hear HIGH sounds.

2. Your teacher will play sounds that go UP or DOWN.
   • Circle the arrow pointing up if the sounds go UP.
   • Circle the arrow pointing down if the sounds go DOWN.

3. Your teacher will clap a rhythm pattern.
   Circle the pattern that you hear.

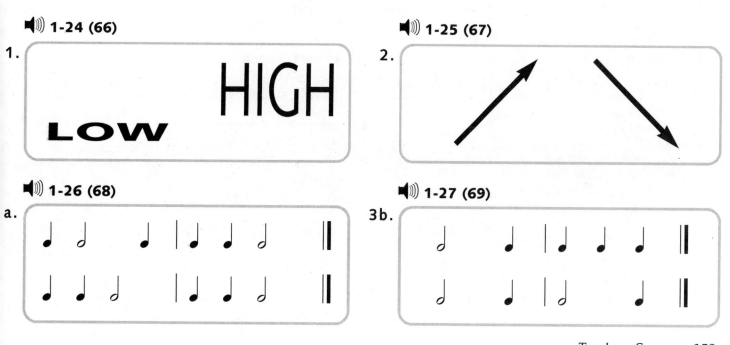

🔊 1-24 (66)

1. LOW / HIGH

🔊 1-25 (67)

2.

🔊 1-26 (68)

a.

🔊 1-27 (69)

3b.

Teacher: See page 153.

Review Worksheet

Name _____   Date _____

1. Write the letter name on each key marked X.

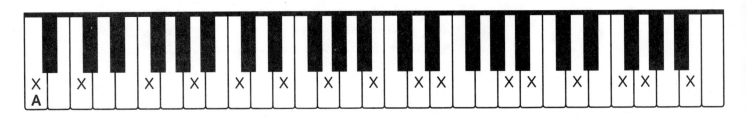

2. Write the numbers from column A in the appropriate blanks
   in column B to match each item with its best description.

Column A	Column B
1. Quarter note ♩	_____ Moderately loud
2. Half note ♩	_____ Note receiving 4 counts
3. Dotted half note ♩.	_____ Soft
4. Whole note 𝅝	_____ Note receiving 1 count
5. Piano *p*	_____ 𝄽
6. Mezzo forte *mf*	_____ ‖
7. Forte *f*	_____ Note receiving 3 counts
8. Quarter rest	_____ Note receiving 2 counts
9. Half rest	_____ Second ending (play second time only)
10. Whole rest	_____ |←———→|←———→|
11. |1.___	_____ ▬
12. |2.___	_____ First ending (play first time only)
13. Repeat sign	_____ ▬
14. Measures and bar lines	_____ Loud
15. Double bar	_____ :‖

Exploring Positions on the Keyboard

UNIT THREE

Objectives

Upon completion of this unit the student will be able to:

1. Identify $\frac{4}{4}$ and $\frac{3}{4}$ time signatures and apply them to performance at the keyboard.

2. Play melodies in Middle C Position, C Position, G Position and other white key positions.

Assignments

Week of _____

Write your assignments for the week in the space below.

_____

_____

_____

_____

_____

_____

_____

_____

_____

_____

_____

_____

_____

_____

_____

Did You Know?

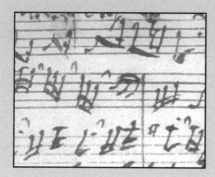

Music Theory

Music theory is the study of the science and inner workings of music. Knowledge of music theory will help you discover how music is put together and how the elements of music function. The basic elements of western music include rhythm, melody and harmony. Learning to play the piano is one of the most effective ways to learn music theory. A careful study of music theory is integrated throughout this book in the music as well as in written work, ear training examples and technical exercises. Analyzing and listening carefully to music will help you better understand how it works.

Playing in Right Hand Middle C Position

Time Signature

Music has numbers at the beginning called a **time signature.**

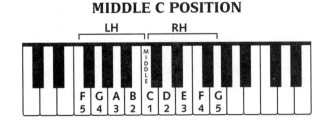

$\frac{4}{4}$ means 4 beats to each measure.

$\frac{4}{4}$ means a **QUARTER NOTE** ♩ gets 1 beat.

READING

MIDDLE C POSITION

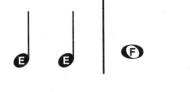

All Through the Night

🔊 **1-28 (70)**

RH Middle C Position

Traditional

Repeat Sign: play again.

Gentle

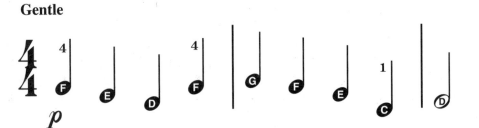

OPTIONAL: Play *All Through the Night* with the LH beginning with finger 2.

TEACHER ACCOMPANIMENT

with pedal

Playing in Left Hand Middle C Position

Time Signature

3 means 3 beats to each measure.

4 means a **QUARTER NOTE** ♩ gets 1 beat.

SOLO REPERTOIRE

First Waltz

🔊 **1-29 (71)**

E. L. Lancaster
Kenon D. Renfrow

LH Middle C Position

Moderately fast

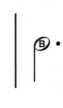

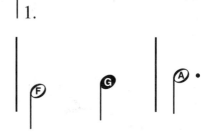

OPTIONAL: Play *First Waltz* with the RH beginning with finger 5.

TEACHER ACCOMPANIMENT

Moderately fast (♩ = 190)

with pedal

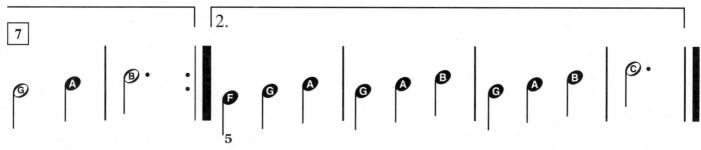

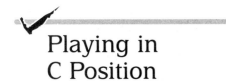

Playing in C Position

1. Play *God Is So Good* with the RH using the fingering above the notes. (The RH uses the same position as Middle C Position.)
2. Play *God Is So Good* with the LH using the fingering below the notes.

C POSITION

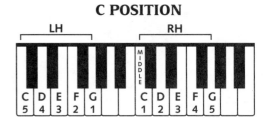

READING

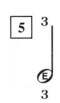 **1-30 (72)**

C Position

God Is So Good

Traditional

Flowing

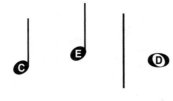

mf

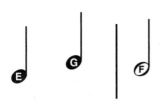

OPTIONAL: Play *God Is So Good* hands together.

TEACHER ACCOMPANIMENT

Playing in G Position

1. Play *Ode to Joy* with the RH using the fingering above the notes.
2. Play *Ode to Joy* with the LH using the fingering below the notes.

READING

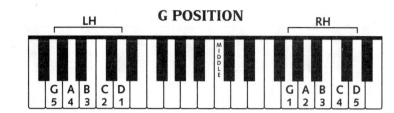

G POSITION

🔊 **1-31 (73)**

G Position

Ode to Joy
(Theme from 9th Symphony)

Ludwig van Beethoven
(1770–1827)

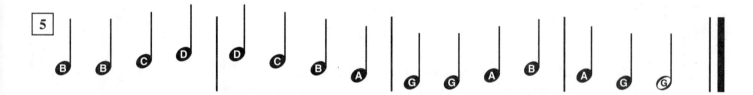

OPTIONAL: Play *Ode to Joy* hands together.

TEACHER ACCOMPANIMENT

Joyful (♩ = 152)

with pedal

Positions Using All
White Keys Moving Up

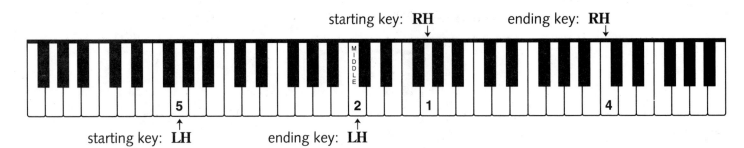

starting key: **RH**   ending key: **RH**

starting key: **LH**   ending key: **LH**

TECHNIQUE

🔊 **1-32 (74)**

1. Play LH alone.
2. Play RH alone.

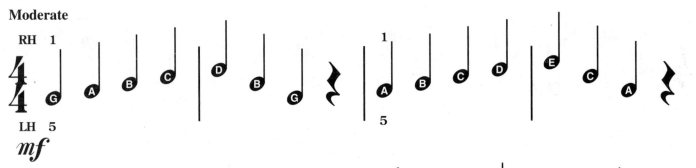

Continue upward
beginning on white keys
until…

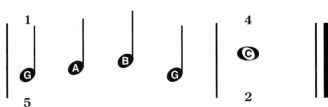

OPTIONAL: Play hands together.

TEACHER ACCOMPANIMENT

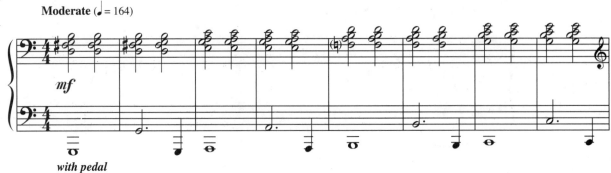

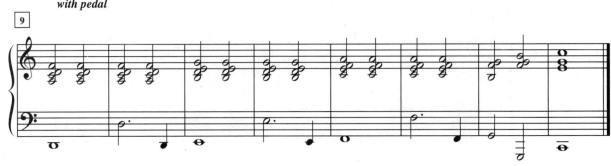

Positions Using All White Keys Moving Down

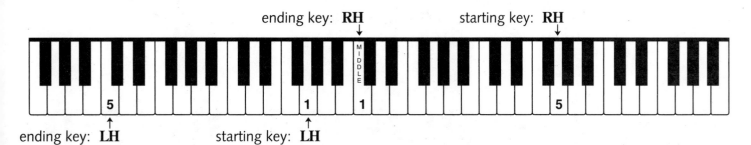

ending key: **RH**   starting key: **RH**

ending key: **LH**   starting key: **LH**

TECHNIQUE

1. Play RH alone.
2. Play LH alone.

🔊 **1-33 (75)**

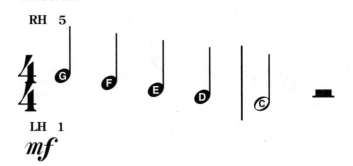

Moderate

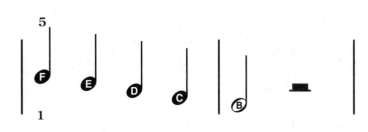

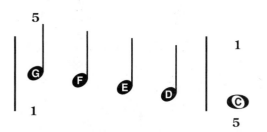

Continue downward beginning on white keys until…

OPTIONAL: Play hands together.

TEACHER ACCOMPANIMENT

Moderate (♩ = 164)

mf

with pedal

Play LH alone two times. Use fingers 1, 2, 3 the first time.
Use fingers 2, 3, 4 the second time.

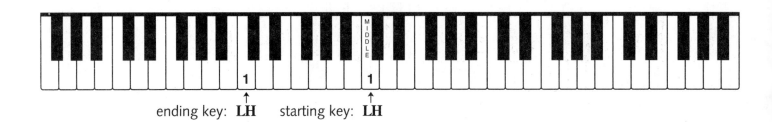

ending key: **LH**   starting key: **LH**

🔊 **1-34 (76)**

With energy

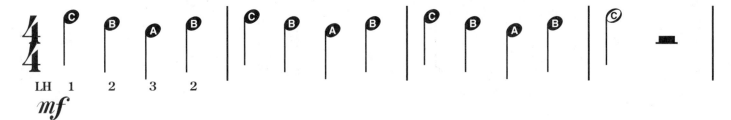

LH   1   2   3   2

mf

5

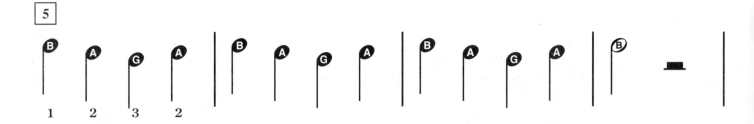

1   2   3   2

Continue downward beginning on white keys until...

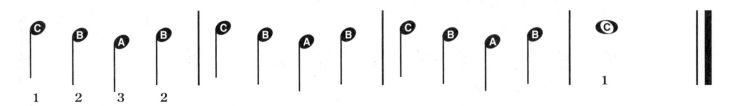

1   2   3   2

1

OPTIONAL: Play hands together.

Play RH alone two times. Use fingers 1, 2, 3 the first time.
Use fingers 2, 3, 4 the second time.

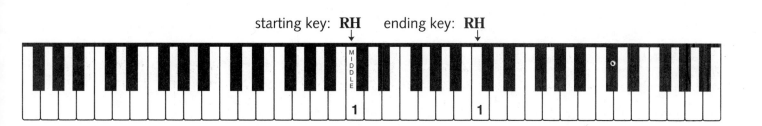

🔊 **1-35 (77)**

With energy

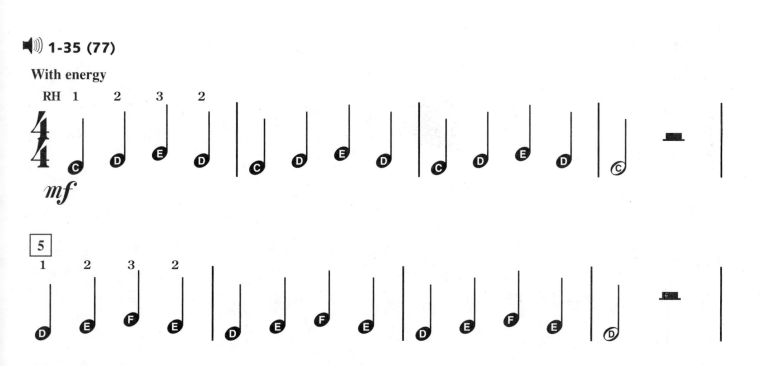

Continue upward beginning on white keys until...

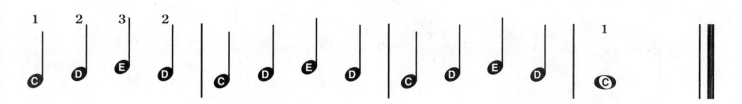

OPTIONAL: Play hands together.

The Staff

✔ Objectives

Upon completion of this unit the student will be able to:

1. Perform solo repertoire from Grand Staff notation.
2. Apply additional musical concepts (crescendo, diminuendo, common time, slurs, legato, phrase) to performance at the keyboard.
3. Identify steps and skips on the staff and perform them on the keyboard.

✔ Assignments

Week of _____

Write your assignments for the week in the space below.

_____

_____

_____

_____

_____

_____

_____

_____

_____

_____

_____

_____

_____

_____

Did You Know?

Musical Style Periods

Musical style results from the interaction of rhythm, melody and harmony. The manner in which one performs keyboard music varies according to the musical style period in which it was composed. There are four basic musical style periods that encompass all of the literature written for piano. Each style period has certain distinguishing characteristics that are unique to that period in music history. In the following units, you will be introduced to the Baroque, Classical, Romantic and Contemporary periods of music history and to some of the composers and compositions written for the piano during the last 300 years.

The Staff

Music is written on a **staff** of 5 lines and 4 spaces. Some notes are written on lines and some are written in spaces.

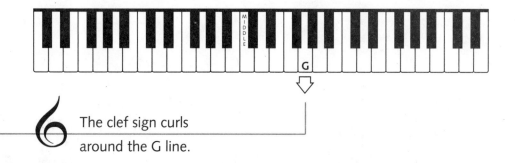

The Treble Clef Sign

The **treble clef** sign locates the G above the middle of the keyboard. This sign came from the letter G.

By moving up or down from this G, you can name any note on the treble staff.

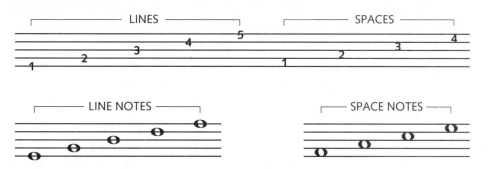

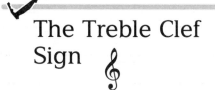

The clef sign curls around the G line.

The Bass Clef Sign

The **bass clef** sign locates the F below the middle of the keyboard. This sign came from the letter F.

By moving up or down from this F, you can name any note on the bass staff.

The F line passes between the two dots of the F clef sign.

The Grand Staff

The bass staff and the treble staff are joined together by a **brace** to make the **grand staff.** A **leger line** is used between the two staves for middle C. Leger lines are also used above and below the grand staff to extend its range.

The notes with arrows are landmarks or guideposts. Learn to identify and find them quickly on the keyboard, as they assist in reading the notes surrounding them.

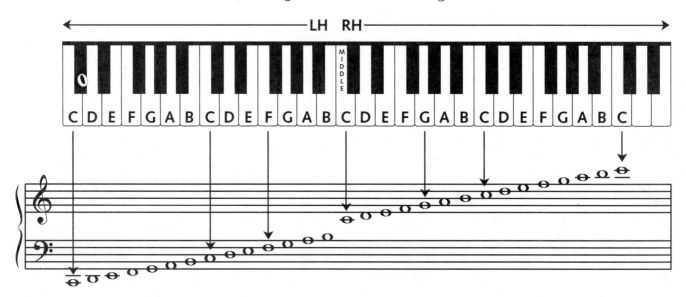

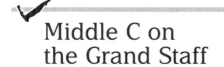

Middle C on the Grand Staff

Middle C appears on a leger line between the treble clef and bass clef. It can be played with either RH or LH.

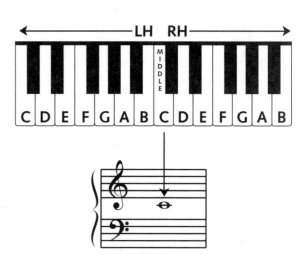

New Dynamic Signs

crescendo (cresc.)

(gradually louder)

diminuendo (dim.) or **decrescendo (decresc.)**

(gradually softer)

New Time Signature

$\mathbf{C}$ = **common time** or $\frac{4}{4}$

READING

Gradual C

🔊 **1-36 (78)**

Steady

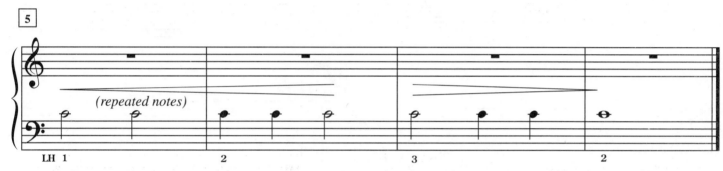

*Notice the fingering changes on the repeated notes. These changes can aid with the crescendo and diminuendo.

TEACHER ACCOMPANIMENT

Steady ($\bullet$ = 164)

with pedal

F Below Middle C

The two dots in the bass clef sign that surround line four locate the F below middle C.

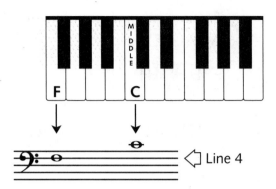

◁ Line 4

READING

🔊 1-37 (79)

F Below

TEACHER ACCOMPANIMENT

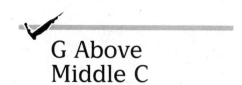

G Above Middle C

The treble clef sign locates the G above middle C by circling line two.

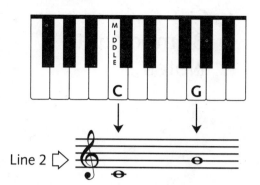

Line 2 ⟹

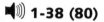

READING

🔊 1-38 (80)

G Above

Moderate

TEACHER ACCOMPANIMENT

Moderate (♩ = 172)

with pedal

3 Important Notes

Write the name of each note on the line below the staff.

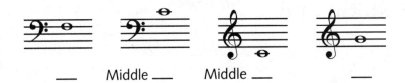

—   Middle —   Middle —   —

READING

🔊 1-39 (81)

Fiddle Tune

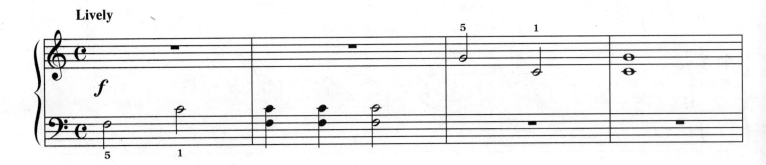

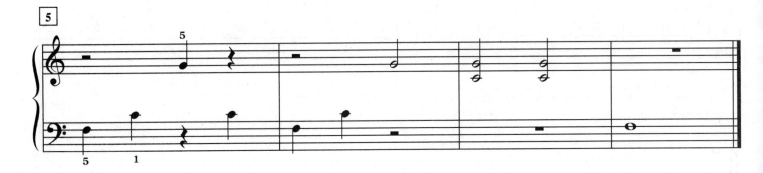

TEACHER ACCOMPANIMENT

Right Hand C Position and Right Hand Middle C Position

The RH C Position consists of **Middle C,** three new notes **D E F** and the **G** above Middle C.

A **STEP** is the distance from any *line* note to the very next *space* note above or below it—or from any *space* note to the very next *line* note above or below it.

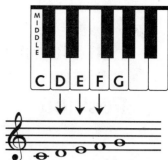

Circle the repeated notes in *One Step at a Time.* All other notes move in steps.

◀))) **1-40 (82)**

One Step at a Time

Moderate

TEACHER ACCOMPANIMENT

Moderate (♩ = 146)

with pedal

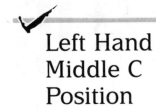

Left Hand Middle C Position

The LH Middle C Position consists of **Middle C,** three new notes **G A B** and the **F** below Middle C.

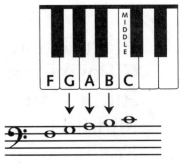

A **SKIP** is the distance from any *space* note to the very next *space* note above or below it—or from any *line* note to the very next *line* note.

READING

Circle seven skips in *Skip Around.*

🔊 **1-41 (83)**

Skip Around

Relaxed

TEACHER ACCOMPANIMENT

Slur & Legato Playing

A **slur** is a curved line over or under notes on *different* lines or spaces. Slurs mean play **legato** (smoothly connected).

Slurs often divide the music into **phrases.** A phrase is a musical thought or sentence.

READING

1-42 (84)

Waltzing Alone

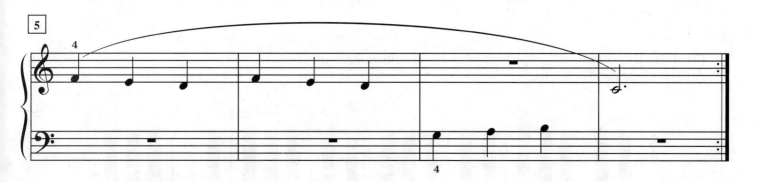

TEACHER ACCOMPANIMENT

Review Worksheet

Name _____   Date _____

1. Print the letter names for both the left hand and right hand
   C POSITION on the keyboard.

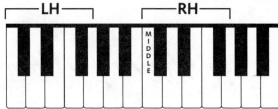

2. Print the letter names for both the left hand and right hand
   MIDDLE C POSITION on the keyboard.

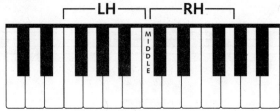

3. Print the letter names for both the left hand and right hand
   G POSITION on the keyboard.

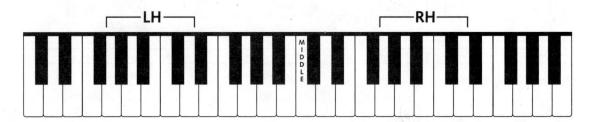

4. Write the name of each note in the square below it—then play
   and say the note names.

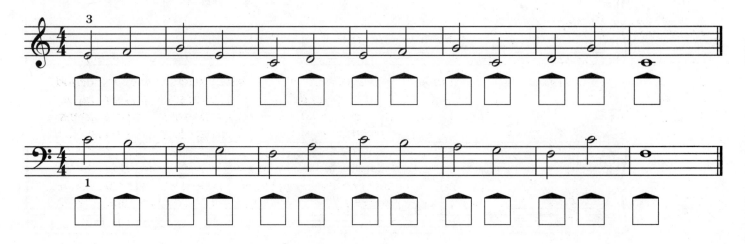

Intervals

Objectives

Upon completion of this unit the student will be able to:

1. Identify melodic and harmonic intervals of 2nds, 3rds, 4ths and 5ths in C Position on the staff and perform them on the keyboard.
2. Identify Italian tempo marks (allegro, moderato, andante) and apply them to performance at the keyboard.
3. Apply additional musical concepts (incomplete measure, tied notes) to performance at the keyboard.
4. Tap two-part rhythm patterns.
5. Aurally distinguish intervals of 2nds, 3rds, 4ths and 5ths in C Position.

Assignments

Week of _____

Write your assignments for the week in the space below.

_____

_____

_____

_____

_____

_____

_____

_____

_____

_____

_____

_____

Did You Know?

The Baroque Period

The Baroque period in music history usually refers to the time period from 1600 to 1750. During this time, the dance suite, prelude, fugue, toccata, and theme and variations were the prevalent musical forms. Much Baroque keyboard music is characterized by two or more lines being played simultaneously to create counterpoint. The harpsichord, clavichord and organ were the primary keyboard instruments of the period. Well-known composers from this period are Johann Sebastian Bach, Domenico Scarlatti, Jean-Philippe Rameau and Antonio Vivaldi.

Left Hand C Position

The left hand C Position has three new notes: **C D E.**

5 4 3 2 1   1 2 3 4 5

READING

Circle the skip in *Gliding Alone.* All other notes move in steps.

 2-1 (39)

Gliding Alone

Moderate

TEACHER ACCOMPANIMENT

Moderate (♩ = 172)

with pedal

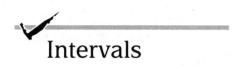

Intervals

Distances between tones are measured in **intervals,** called 2nds, 3rds, 4ths, 5ths, etc.

- The distance from any white key to the next white key, up or down, is called a 2nd.
- When you skip a white key, the interval is a 3rd.
- When you skip two white keys, the interval is a 4th.
- When you skip three white keys, the interval is a 5th.

Melodic Intervals

Notes played separately make a melody. The intervals between these notes are called **melodic intervals.**

◀))) 2-2 (40)

Listen to the sound of each interval as you play these melodic 2nds, 3rds, 4ths and 5ths.

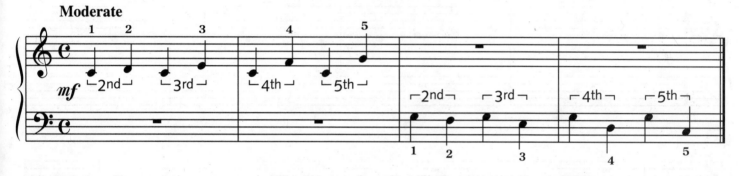

Harmonic Intervals

Notes played together make harmony. The intervals between these notes are called **harmonic intervals.**

◀))) 2-3 (41)

Listen to the sound of each interval as you play these harmonic 2nds, 3rds, 4ths and 5ths.

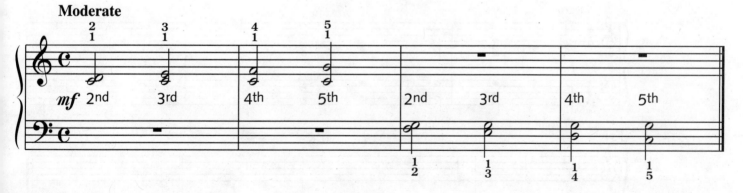

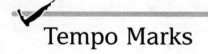

Tempo Marks

Tempo is an Italian word that means "rate of speed." Words indicating the tempo used in playing music are called **tempo marks.**

Some of the most important tempo marks are:

Allegro	=	Quickly, happily
Moderato	=	Moderately
Andante	=	Moving along (The word actually means "walking.")
Adagio	=	Slowly

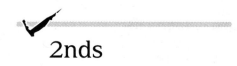

2nds

The distance from any white key to the next white key, up or down, is called a **2nd.**

2nds go from *line* to *space* or from *space* to *line*:

Line to space   Space to line

READING

Notice the melodic 2nds in measures 1 and 5 of *Ode to Joy.*
Place brackets over the 2nds in the remainder of the piece.

Ode to Joy
(Theme from 9th Symphony)

Ludwig van Beethoven
(1770–1827)

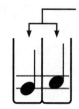 2-4 (42)

TEACHER ACCOMPANIMENT

Transposition

Ode to Joy was played in the **G Position** on page 23.
Here it is played in the **C Position.**

Playing music in a different key from the original
is called **transposition.**

3rds

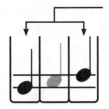

When you skip a white key, the interval is a **3rd**.

3rds go from *line* to *line* or from *space* to *space*:

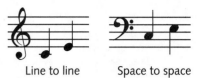

Line to line   Space to space

New Dynamic Sign

mp *(mezzo piano)* = moderately soft

READING

Notice the melodic 3rds in measures 1 and 5 of *Love Somebody*. Place brackets over the 3rds in the remainder of the piece.

Love Somebody

🔊 **2-5 (43)**

Traditional

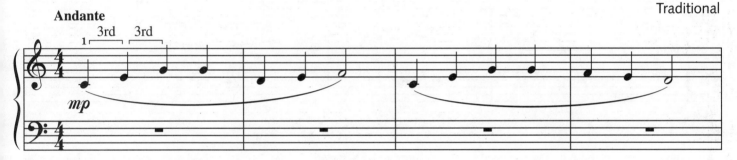

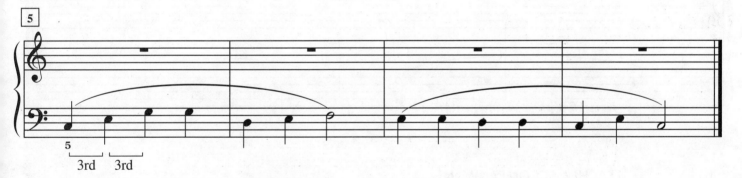

TEACHER ACCOMPANIMENT

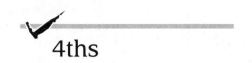

4ths

When you skip 2 white keys, the interval is a **4th**.

4ths go from
line to *space* or
from *space* to *line*:

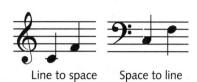

Line to space   Space to line

READING

Notice the melodic 4ths in measures 1 and 5 of *Aura Lee*.
Place brackets over the 4ths in the remainder of the piece.

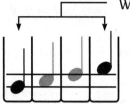

Aura Lee

🔊 2-6 (44)

Moderato

Traditional

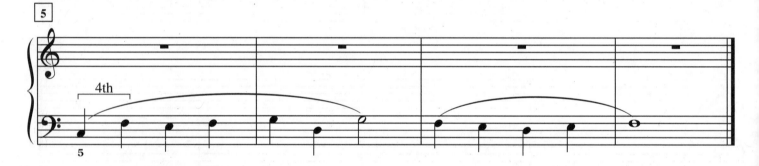

TEACHER ACCOMPANIMENT

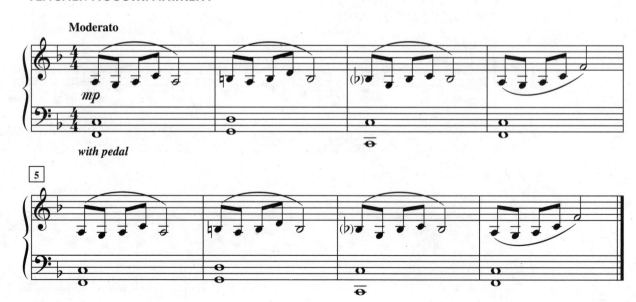

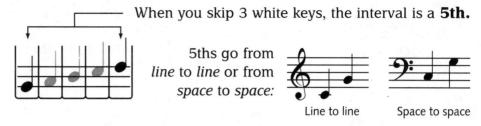

When you skip 3 white keys, the interval is a **5th.**

5ths go from
line to *line* or from
space to *space:*

Line to line   Space to space

✔
Tied Notes

When notes on the same line or space are joined by a curved line, we call them tied notes (♩‿♩). The key is held down for the combined values of both notes.

READING

Notice the melodic and harmonic 5ths in the first line of *Fifth Wheel.* Identify the 5ths in the remainder of the piece.

Fifth Wheel

🔊 2-7 (45)

TEACHER ACCOMPANIMENT

Incomplete Measure

Some pieces begin with an incomplete measure. The first measure of *Interval Study* has only three counts. It begins on beat 2. The one missing count is found in the last measure.

READING

On the lines below the staff, write the name (2nd, 3rd, 4th or 5th) of each harmonic interval in the left hand.

Interval Study

🔊 **2-8 (46)**

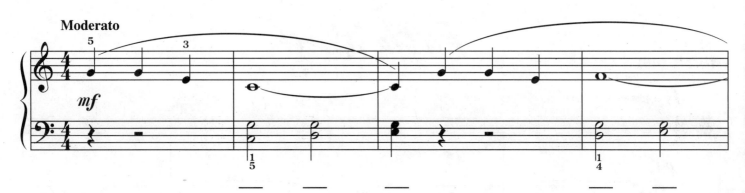

TEACHER ACCOMPANIMENT

Identify the harmonic intervals in the LH of *When the Saints Go Marching In.*

When the Saints Go Marching In

2-9 (47)

Traditional
arr. E. L. Lancaster & Kenon D. Renfrow

TEACHER ACCOMPANIMENT

RHYTHM READING

Tap the following rhythm patterns using RH for notes with stems going up and LH for notes with stems going down. Tap hands separately first, and then hands together, always counting aloud.

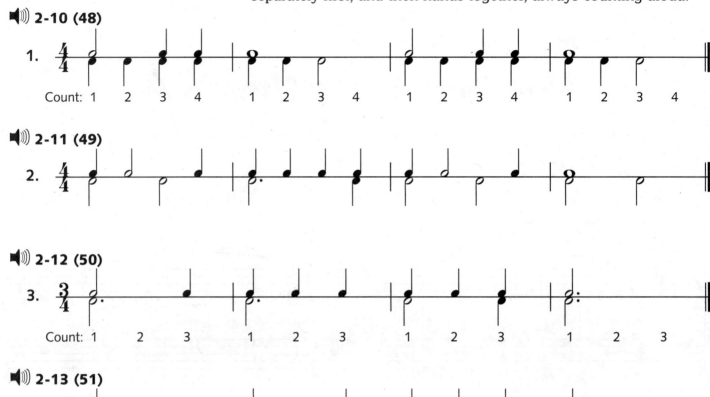

🔊 2-10 (48)

1.

Count: 1 2 3 4   1 2 3 4   1 2 3 4   1 2 3 4

🔊 2-11 (49)

2.

🔊 2-12 (50)

3.

Count: 1 2 3   1 2 3   1 2 3   1 2 3

🔊 2-13 (51)

4.

EAR TRAINING

1. Your teacher will play intervals of a 2nd or 4th. Circle the interval that you hear.

2. Your teacher will play intervals of a 3rd or 5th. Circle the interval that you hear.

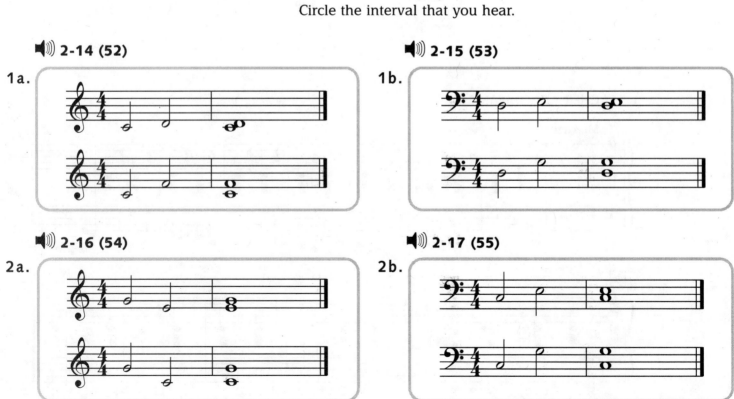

🔊 2-14 (52)

1a.

🔊 2-15 (53)

1b.

🔊 2-16 (54)

2a.

🔊 2-17 (55)

2b.

Teacher: See page 153.

Review Worksheet

Name _____   Date _____

1. Write a half note below the given note to make the indicated *melodic* interval.
   Turn all the stems in the treble clef UP.

   Turn all the stems in the bass clef DOWN. Write the name of each note in the square below it.

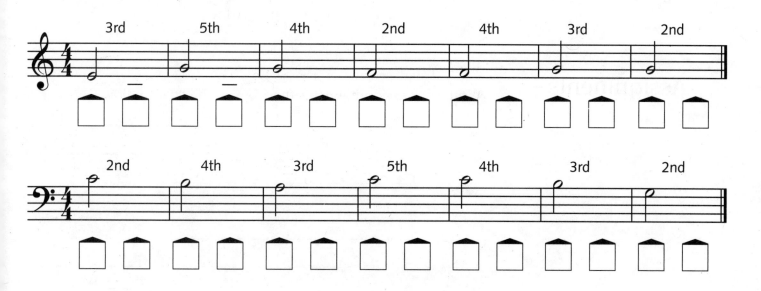

2. Write a whole note above the given note to make the indicated *harmonic* interval.
   Write the names of the notes in the squares.

   Write the name of the lower note in the lower square; the name of the higher note in the higher square.

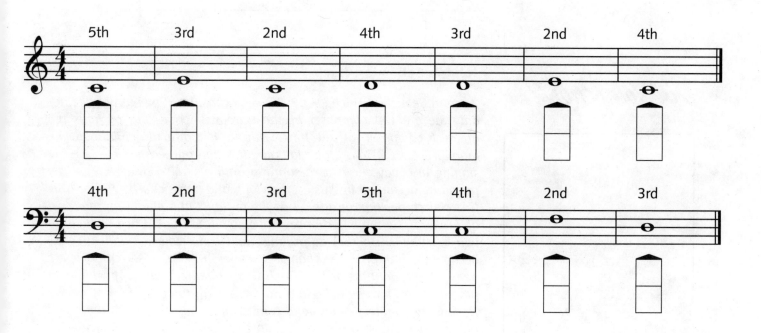

Other Keyboard Basics

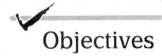

Objectives

Upon completion of this unit the student will be able to:

1. Identify additional musical concepts (sharp signs, flat signs, staccato marks, $\frac{2}{4}$ time signature, ritardando, adagio, D.C. al Fine) and apply them to performance at the keyboard.

2. Expand the reading range by playing in C Position an octave higher in the right hand.

3. Perform duet repertoire with a partner.

Assignments

Week of _____

Write your assignments for the week in the space below.

_____

_____

_____

_____

_____

_____

_____

_____

_____

_____

_____

_____

Did You Know?

Johann Sebastian Bach

Johann Sebastian Bach (1685–1750) is considered by many to be not only the greatest composer of the Baroque period, but perhaps the greatest composer of all time. During his difficult childhood, he managed to receive a broad liberal education and earned his keep by singing in a boy choir (as a soprano until his voice changed) and by providing accompaniments on the violin and harpsichord. He took his first church position at age 18 as the organist at a church in the town of Arnstadt, Germany. After several church positions, Bach worked for two wealthy aristocrats as organist and concertmaster and in 1723 became the Cantor of St. Thomas's School in Leipzig, Germany, where he remained until his death. Bach wrote hundreds of compositions in practically all forms of the late Baroque, with the exception of opera. Bach is the greatest example of a musical genius who consistently did his job to the best of his ability, to satisfy his employer, educate his peers and to glorify God.

The Sharp Sign

The **sharp sign** before a note means play the next key to the *right*, whether black or white.

When a sharp appears before a note, it applies to that note for the rest of the measure.

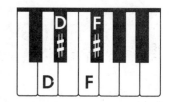

SOLO REPERTOIRE

Money Can't Buy Ev'rything!

2-18 (56)

Willard A. Palmer, Morton Manus
and Amanda Vick Lethco

The Flat Sign

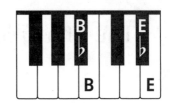

The **flat sign** before a note means play the next key to the *left*, whether black or white.

When a flat appears before a note, it applies to that note for the rest of the measure.

READING

Flat Top

🔊 **2-19 (57)**

TEACHER ACCOMPANIMENT

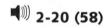

The Natural Sign

The **natural sign** cancels a sharp or flat.

A note after a natural sign is always a white key.

READING

Naturally

🔊 **2-20 (58)**

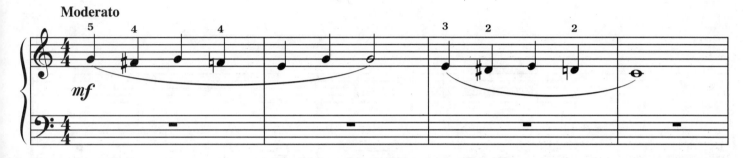

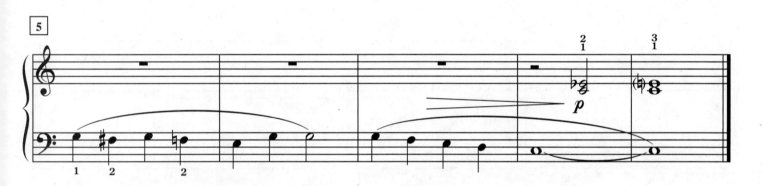

TEACHER ACCOMPANIMENT

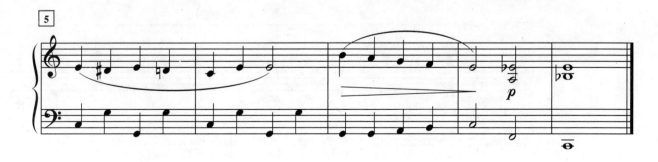

Bright Lights Boogie

2-21 (59)

Gayle Kowalchyk

E. L. Lancaster

With energy

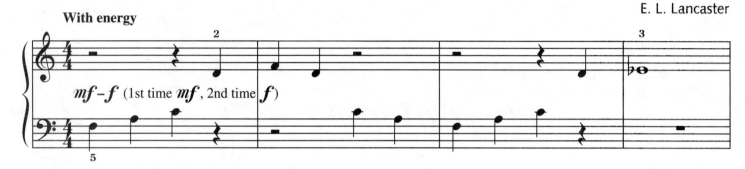

mf–f (1st time *mf*, 2nd time *f*)

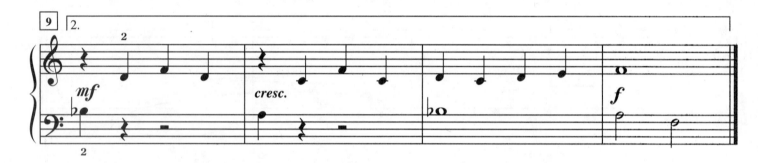

TEACHER ACCOMPANIMENT (Student plays 1 octave higher)

"Bright Lights Boogie" from BOOGIE 'N' BLUES, BOOK 1, by Gayle Kowalchyk and E. L. Lancaster
Copyright © MCMXCI by Alfred Publishing Co., Inc.

Right Hand C Position
an Octave Higher

The RH C Position can be played an octave higher (new notes **C D E F** and **G**).

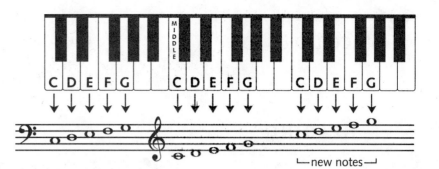

└─new notes─┘

READING

🔊 **2-22 (60)**

Remember

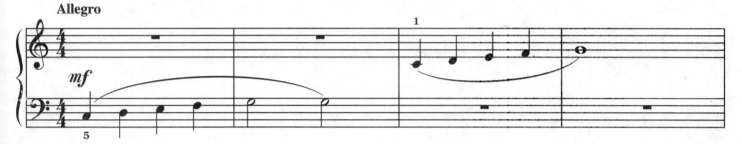

Allegro

mf

5

RH move

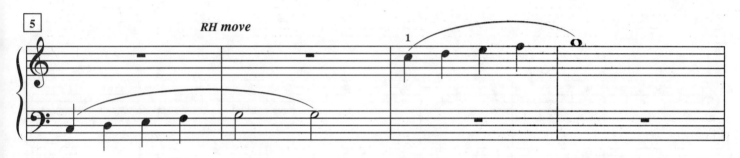

9

RH move   *LH over*

TEACHER ACCOMPANIMENT

Allegro

mf

with pedal

7

Staccato

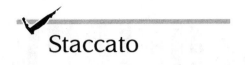

The dot over or under the notes indicates the staccato touch. Make these notes very short!

Short Drive

🔊 **2-23 (61)**

TEACHER ACCOMPANIMENT

New Time Signature

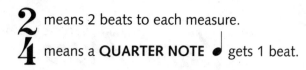

$\frac{2}{4}$ means 2 beats to each measure.

means a **QUARTER NOTE** ♩ gets 1 beat.

New Tempo Mark

Allegretto = moderately fast

**READING**

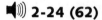 2-24 (62)

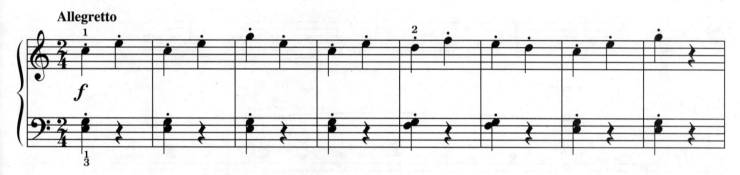

TEACHER ACCOMPANIMENT

Lyric Piece
from *The Children's Musical Friend*

🔊 **2-25 (63)**

Heinrich Wohlfahrt (1797–1883)
Op. 87, No. 27

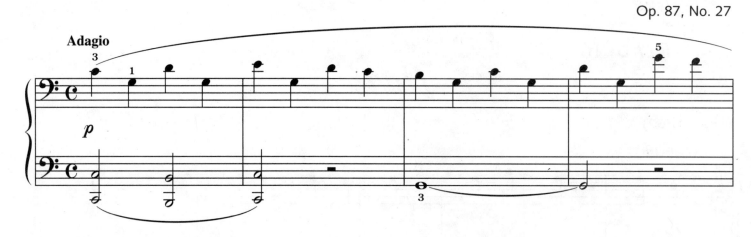

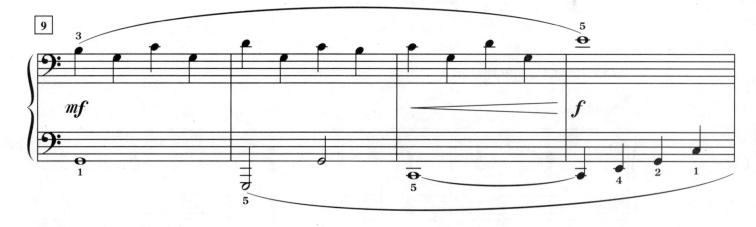

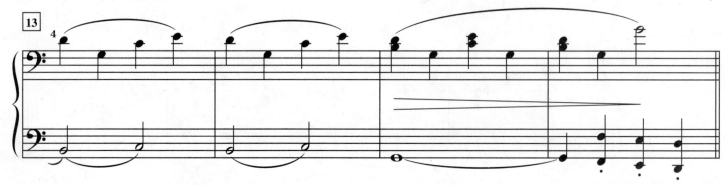

D.C. al Fine

Student

Lyric Piece

from *The Children's Musical Friend*

🔊 **2-25 (63)**

Heinrich Wohlfahrt (1797–1883)
Op. 87, No. 27

Adagio
(Both hands two octaves higher than written throughout)

rit. (ritardando)
gradually slowing

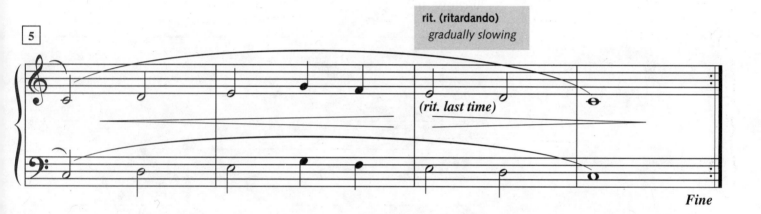

(rit. last time)

Fine

D.C. (da capo) al Fine
*repeat from the beginning
and play to Fine (the end).*

D.C. al Fine

G Position

Objectives

Upon completion of this unit the student will be able to:

1. Expand the reading range by playing in G Position and in G Position an octave higher in the left hand.

2. Identify additional musical concepts (accent sign, pianissimo) and apply them to performance at the keyboard.

3. Identify melodic and harmonic intervals of 2nds, 3rds, 4ths and 5ths on the staff, and perform them on the keyboard.

4. Tap two-part rhythm patterns.

5. Aurally distinguish intervals of 2nds, 3rds, 4ths and 5ths in G Position.

Assignments

Week of _____

Write your assignments for the week in the space below.

_____

_____

_____

_____

_____

_____

_____

_____

_____

_____

Did You Know?

Church Music

*W*estern music as we know it grew out of the early church. The practice of singing during religious services can be traced back to ancient Jewish temples. Portions of the Book of Psalms, written as early as 1,400 years before Christ, refer specifically to singing. As the liturgy of the church later became standardized, almost all faiths began singing these liturgies in plainchant. Plainchant, which later became known as Gregorian chant (named after Pope Gregory the Great), was the first type of music to be written down using a primitive system of notation. During the Reformation in Germany in the early 16th century, the Lutheran church began singing hymns as we know them today. The church is still one of the most accessible venues for amateur musicians to sing and make music.

G Position on the Staff

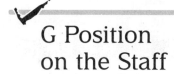

New notes are **G A B** in bass clef; **A B** in treble clef.

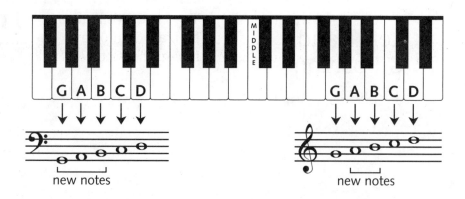

Accent Sign

An accent sign over or under a note means play that note louder.

2-26 (64)

Midnight Shadows

E. L. Lancaster

Mysteriously

dim. to end

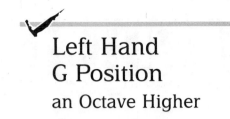

Left Hand
G Position
an Octave Higher

The LH G Position can be played an octave higher (new note **D**).

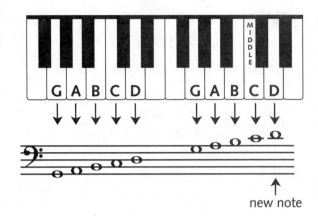

new note

R E A D I N G

Summer Fun

🔊 **2-27 (65)**

TEACHER ACCOMPANIMENT

Intervals in G Position

Melodic Intervals

Listen to the sound of each interval as you play these melodic 2nds, 3rds, 4ths and 5ths.

1.
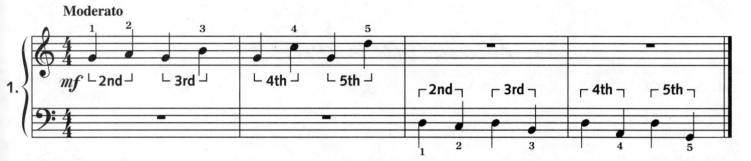

2.
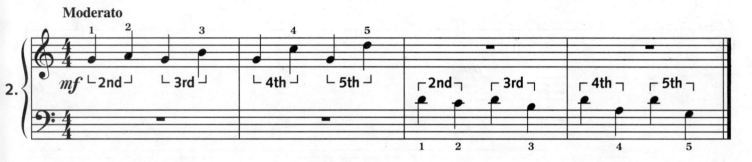

Harmonic Intervals

Listen to the sound of each interval as you play these harmonic 2nds, 3rds, 4ths and 5ths.

3.

4.
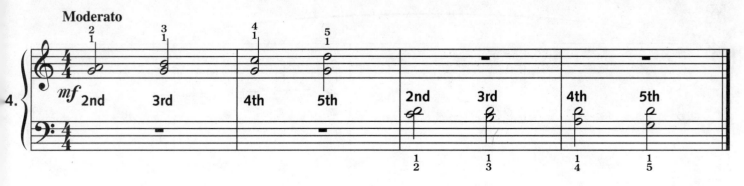

New Dynamic Sign

pp *(pianissimo)* = very soft

SOLO REPERTOIRE

Miniature Waltz

🔊 **2-30 (68)**

E. L. Lancaster
Kenon D. Renfrow

RHYTHM READING

Tap the following rhythm patterns using RH for notes with stems going up and LH for notes with stems going down. Tap hands separately first, and then hands together, always counting aloud.

🔊 **2-31 (69)**

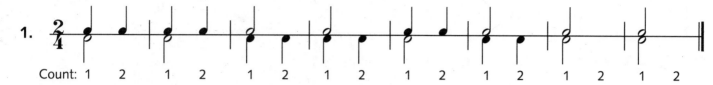

Count: 1   2   1   2   1   2   1   2   1   2   1   2   1   2   1   2

🔊 **2-32 (70)**

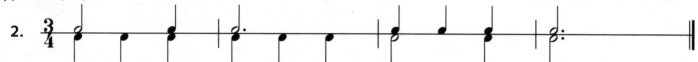

🔊 **2-33 (71)**

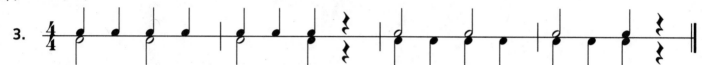

🔊 **2-34 (72)**

EAR TRAINING

1. Your teacher will play intervals of a 2nd or 4th. Circle the interval that you hear.

2. Your teacher will play intervals of a 3rd or 5th. Circle the interval that you hear.

🔊 **2-35 (73)**

a.

🔊 **2-36 (74)**

1b.

🔊 **2-37 (75)**

a.

🔊 **2-38 (76)**

2b.

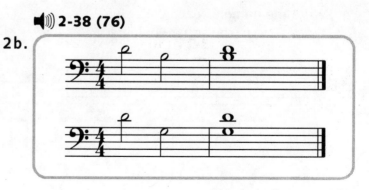

Teacher: See page 153.

Review Worksheet

Name _____

Date _____

You have now learned all the notes on the Grand Staff.

1. Write the name of each treble clef line note in the square below it.

TREBLE CLEF
LINE NOTES

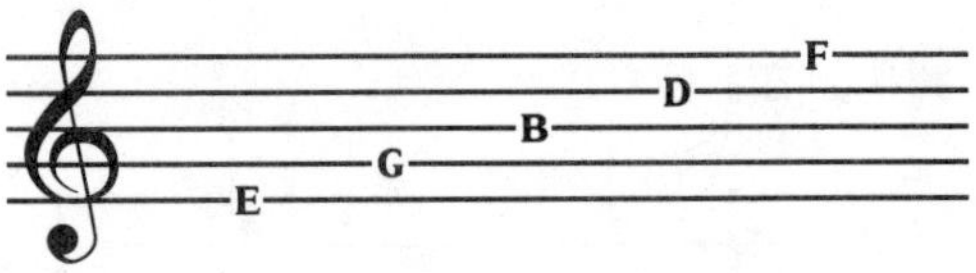

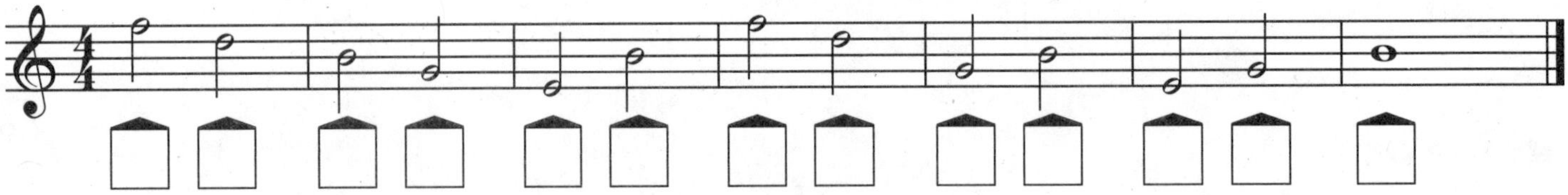

2. Write the name of each treble clef space note in the square below it.

TREBLE CLEF
SPACE NOTES

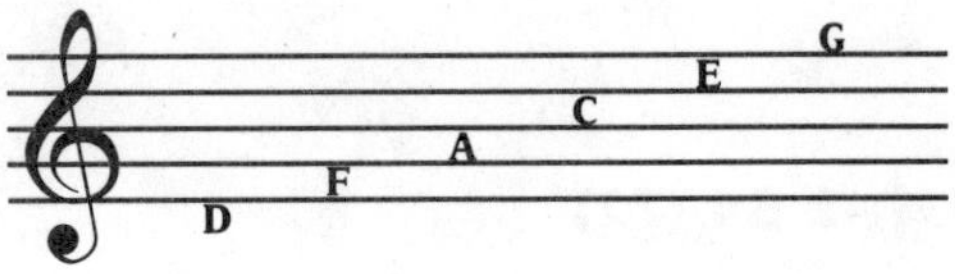

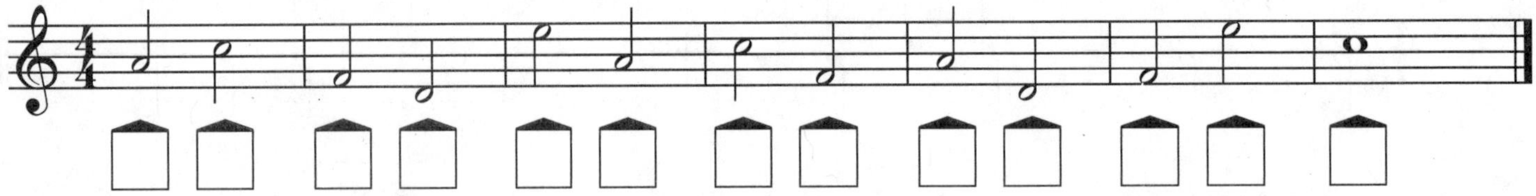

3. Write the name of each bass clef line note in the square below it.

BASS CLEF
LINE NOTES

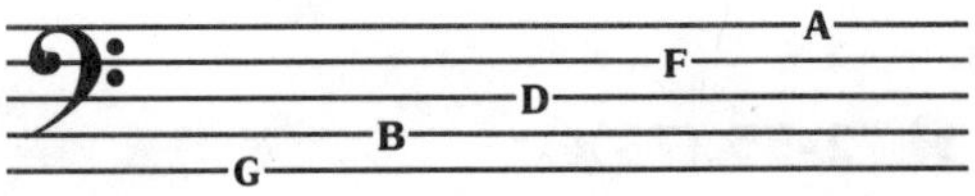

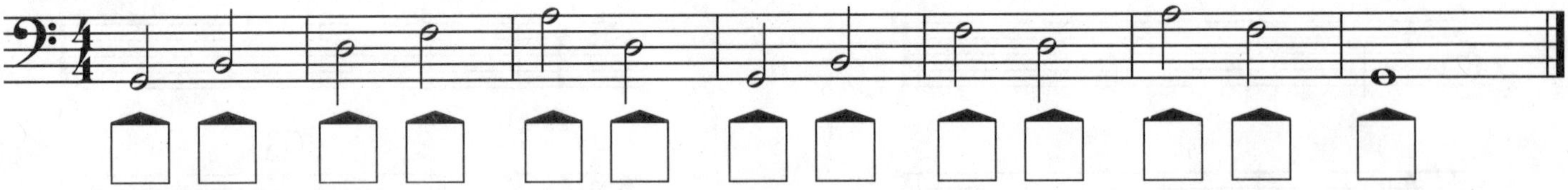

4. Write the name of each bass clef space note in the square below it.

BASS CLEF
SPACE NOTES

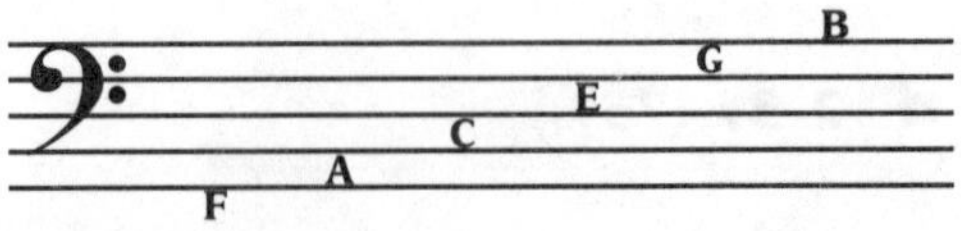

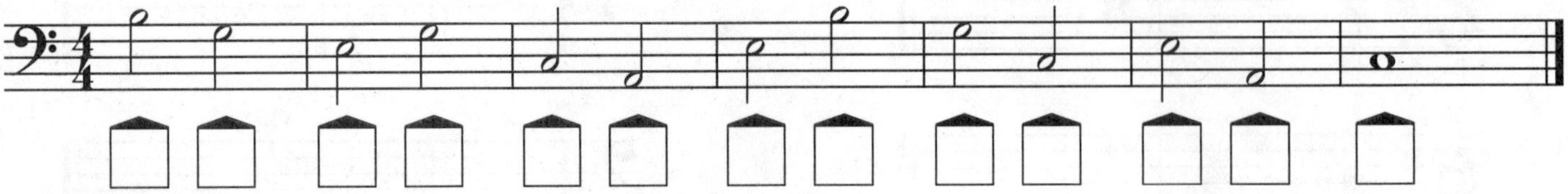

Major Five-Finger Patterns

Objectives

Upon completion of this unit the student will be able to:

1. Identify and play whole steps, half steps and the chromatic scale on the keyboard.
2. Play major five-finger patterns and triads beginning on any white key.
3. Identify additional musical concepts (eighth notes) and apply them to performance at the keyboard.
4. Perform ensemble repertoire with partners.
5. Tap two-part rhythm patterns.

Assignments

Week of _____

Write your assignments for the week in the space below.

_____

_____

_____

_____

_____

_____

_____

_____

_____

_____

_____

_____

_____

_____

Did You Know?

The Classical Period

During the Classical period, from 1750 to 1820, sonata-allegro, minuet and trio, rondo, and theme and variations were the prevalent music forms. Much of the keyboard music from this period is characterized by a single line melody in the right hand while the left hand plays a chordal accompaniment. The fortepiano, harpsichord and organ were the keyboard instruments of the period. Well-known composers from this period are Franz Joseph Haydn, Wolfgang Amadeus Mozart, Muzio Clementi and Ludwig van Beethoven.

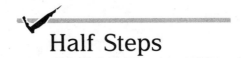

Half Steps

A **half step** is the distance from any key to the very next key above or below it (black or white)—there is no key between.

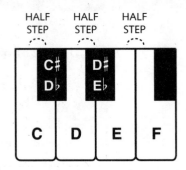

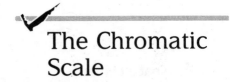

The Chromatic Scale

The **chromatic scale** is made up entirely of half steps. It goes up and down, using every key, black and white. It may begin on any key.

The fingering rules are:

- Use 3 on each black key.
- Use 1 on each white key, except when two white keys are together (no black key between), then use 1 2 or 2 1.

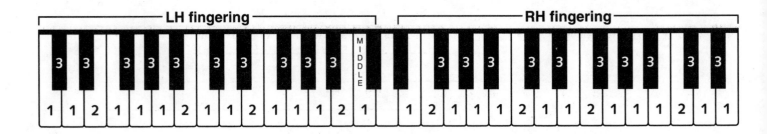

Playing the Chromatic Scale

1. Looking at the keyboard above, play the chromatic scale with the LH. Begin on middle C and go down for two octaves and then go up again.

2. Looking at the keyboard above, play the chromatic scale with the RH. Begin on E above middle C and go up for two octaves and then go down again.

3. By combining steps 1 and 2 above, play the chromatic scale hands together. Notice that each hand plays the same finger at the same time.

A **whole step** is equal to two half steps.
Skip one key (black or white).

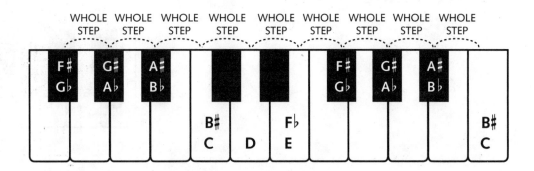

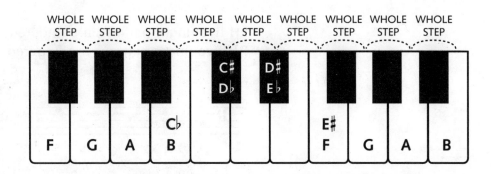

Building Patterns of Whole Steps

Begin on the given key and build an ascending pattern using only whole steps. Write the names of the keys in the blanks. Do not skip or repeat any letters.

1. C ___ ___
2. D ___ ___
3. E ___ ___
4. F ___ ___
5. G ___ ___
6. A ___ ___
7. B ___ ___
8. G♭ ___ ___

9. A♭ ___ ___
10. B♭ ___ ___
11. D♭ ___ ___
12. E♭ ___ ___
13. F♯ ___ ___
14. G♯ ___ ___
15. C♯ ___ ___

Major Five-Finger Patterns

A major five-finger pattern is a series of five notes having the pattern: *whole step, whole step, half step, whole step.*

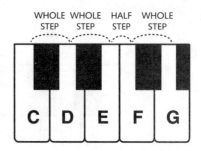

LH five-finger patterns are fingered 5 4 3 2 1.
RH five-finger patterns are fingered 1 2 3 4 5.

WRITTEN EXERCISE

Write letter names on the correct keys to form each major five-finger pattern.

Example:

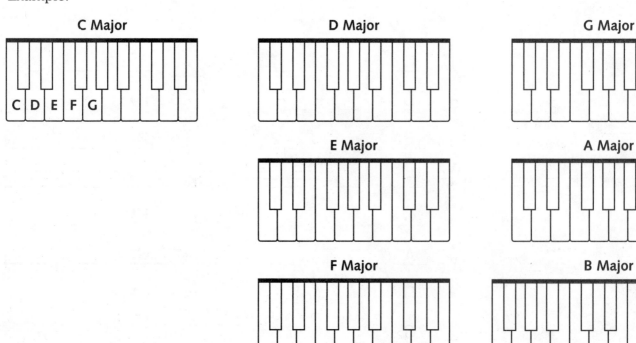

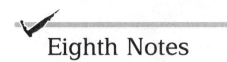

Eighth Notes

Two **eighth notes** are played in the time of one quarter note.

Eighth notes are usually played in pairs.

count: 1 &
or: 2 8ths

When a piece contains eighth notes,

count: 1 - & *or* 2 - 8ths for each pair of eighth notes;

       1 - & for each quarter note;

       1 - & - 2 - & for each half note.

Clap (or tap) these notes, counting aloud.

🔊 **3-1 (30)**

1. [musical notation, 4/4]
Count: 1 & 2 & 3 & 4 & 1 & 2 & 3 & 4 &

🔊 **3-2 (31)**

2. [musical notation, 4/4]

🔊 **3-3 (32)**

3. [musical notation, 3/4]

🔊 **3-4 (33)**

4. [musical notation, 3/4]

Playing Major Five-Finger Patterns

1. Play the following exercise that uses major five-finger patterns.

2. *(Optional)* Play the exercise beginning on D♭. Continue upward beginning on black keys until the next D♭ is reached.

 🔊 **3-5 (34)**

Continue upward beginning on white keys until...

Major Triads (Chords)

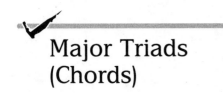

A **triad** is a three-note chord. The three notes of a triad are the root (1), the third (3), and the fifth (5). The **root** is the note from which the triad gets its name. The root of a C triad is C. Triads in root position (with the root at the bottom) always look like this:

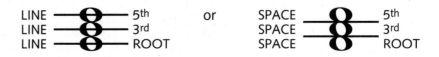

LH triads are fingered 5 3 1. RH triads are fingered 1 3 5.

Playing Major Five-Finger Patterns and Chords

1. Play the following exercise that uses major five-finger patterns and chords.

2. *(Optional)* Play the exercise beginning on D♭. Continue upward beginning on black keys until the next D♭ is reached.

◄))) **3-6 (35)**

Shall We Gather at the River

(D Major Five-Finger Pattern)

Robert Lowry
(1826–1899)

🔊 **3-7 (36)**

TEACHER ACCOMPANIMENT

Forty-Finger Ensemble
(A Major Five-Finger Pattern)

Part 1

3-8 (37)

E. L. Lancaster

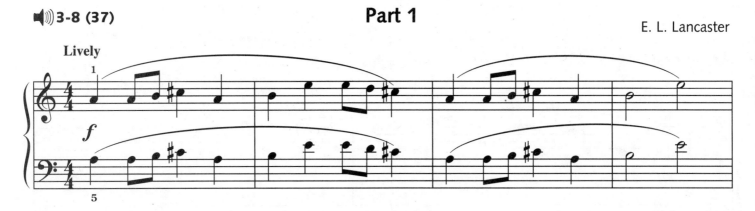

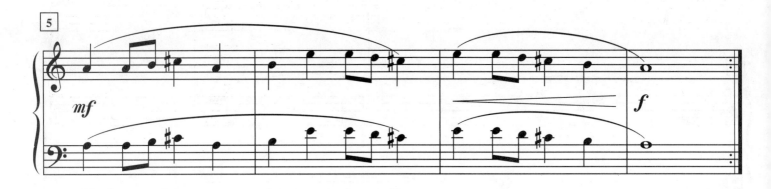

Part 2

3-8 (37)

E. L. Lancaster

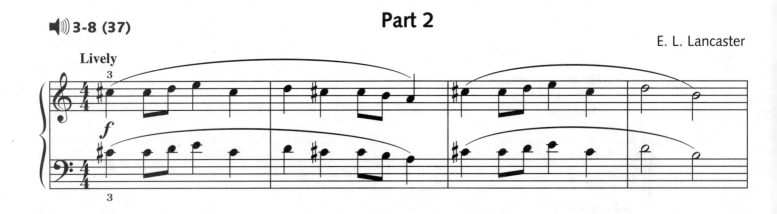

Part 3

Lively

Both hands one octave higher than written throughout

E. L. Lancaster

Part 4

Lively

Both hands two octaves lower than written throughout

E. L. Lancaster

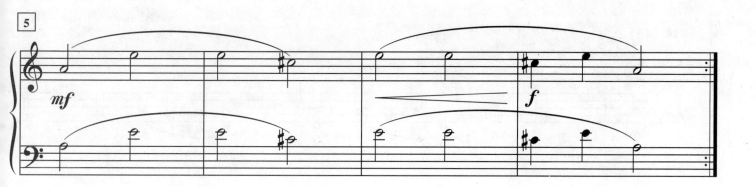

RHYTHM READING

Tap the following rhythm patterns using RH for notes with stems going up and LH for notes with stems going down. Tap hands separately first, and then hands together, always counting aloud.

🔊 **3-9 (38)**

1.

Count: 1 & 2 & 3 & 4 &   1 & 2 & 3 & 4 &   1 & 2 & 3 & 4 &   1 & 2 & 3 & 4 &

🔊 **3-10 (39)**

2.

🔊 **3-11 (40)**

3.

🔊 **3-12 (41)**

4.

TECHNIQUE

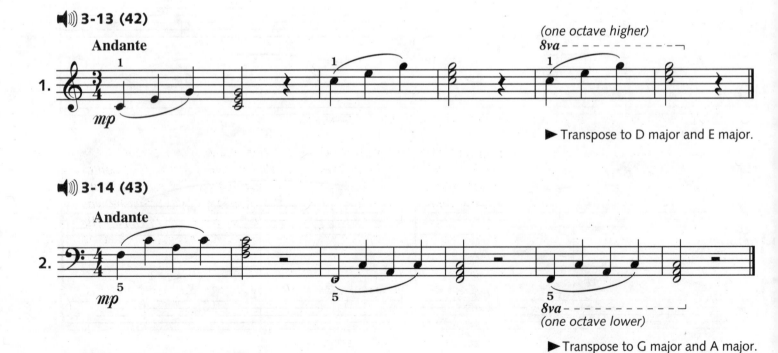

🔊 **3-13 (42)**

Andante

(one octave higher)
8va - - - - - - - - - - - - -

1.

mp

▶ Transpose to D major and E major.

🔊 **3-14 (43)**

Andante

2.

mp

8va - - - - - - - - - - - -
(one octave lower)

▶ Transpose to G major and A major.

Key of C Major

✔ Objectives

Upon completion of this unit the student will be able to:

1. Build major scales beginning on C, G and F.
2. Play the C major scale using traditional fingerings.
3. Build and play the C major, G7 and F major chords in close position in the key of C major.
4. Identify and perform repertoire in **binary** form (AB).

✔ Assignments

Week of _____

Write your assignments for the week in the space below.

_____

_____

_____

_____

_____

_____

_____

_____

_____

_____

_____

_____

_____

_____

_____

Did You Know?

Wolfgang Amadeus Mozart

Wolfgang Amadeus Mozart (1756–1791) is considered to be one of the most creative musical geniuses the world has ever known. The son of a talented musician and teacher, Mozart showed signs of extraordinary musical ability early in life. He began composing music when he was five, and performed for the Austrian empress when he was six. His father recognized Wolfgang's talents and spent much of his time educating the young boy and parading him throughout Europe for concert tours. Mozart thrilled many audiences with his quick wit, his incredible performing ability and his outstanding compositions. Mozart particularly enjoyed playing duets with his sister, Nannerl. Even though he died in poverty at the age of 35, his legacy to the world includes more than 600 compositions.

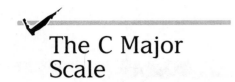

The C Major Scale

The C Major Five-Finger Pattern plus two added notes (A and B) and the C an octave higher form the **C major scale.**

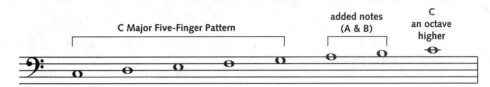

Tetrachords and the Major Scale

Any major scale can be built from two tetrachords.

A **tetrachord** is a series of four notes having a pattern of *whole step, whole step, half step.*

LH tetrachords are fingered 5 4 3 2.
RH tetrachords are fingered 2 3 4 5.

The **major scale** is made of two tetrachords joined by a whole step. Each scale begins and ends on a note of the same name as the scale, called the **key note.** Any major scale can be formed by following this sequence of whole and half steps: W W H W W W H.

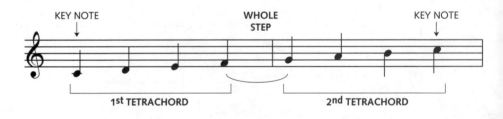

Building and Playing Major Scales

Write letter names on the correct keys to form each major scale. Then play using tetrachord position.

Example:

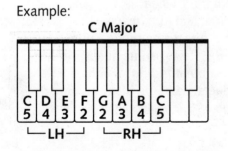

G Major

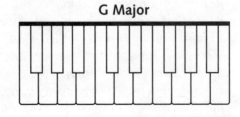

F Major

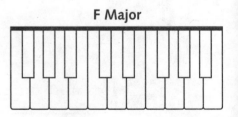

Scale Master

🔊 3-15 (44)

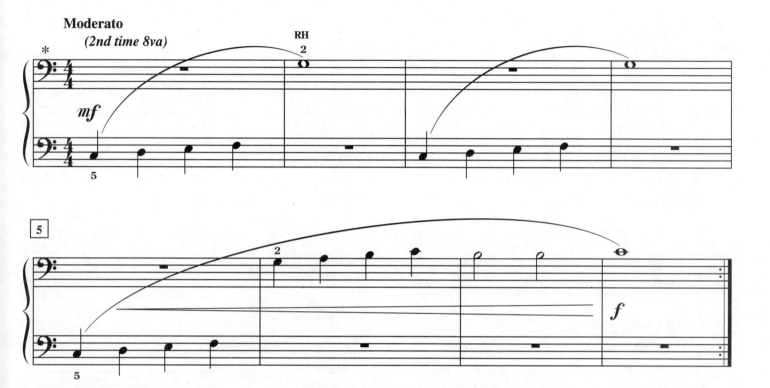

*Note: Both hands read bass clef.

TEACHER ACCOMPANIMENT

Preparation for Scale Playing

🔊 **3-16 (45)**

Moderato

Pass 1 under 3

Cross 3 over 1

1.

mf

🔊 **3-17 (46)**

Moderato

2.

mf

Pass 1 under 3

Cross 3 over 1

🔊 **3-18 (47)**

Moderato

3.

mf

Continue upward on white keys until. . .

🔊 **3-19 (48)**

Moderato

4.

mf

Continue downward on white keys until. . .

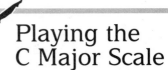

Playing the C Major Scale

Practice slowly hands separately. Lean the hand slightly in the direction you are moving. The hand should move smoothly along with no twisting motion of the wrist!

🔊 **3-20 (49)**

Pass 1 under 3

Cross 3 over 1

RH

🔊 **3-21 (50)**

LH

Pass 1 under 3

Cross 3 over 1

Play the scales above hands together. The RH ascends as the LH descends, and vice versa (in contrary motion). Both hands play the same numbered fingers at the same time.

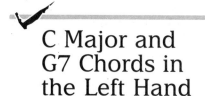

C Major and G7 Chords in the Left Hand

Two frequently used chords are C major and G7.

Chord symbols are always used in popular music to identify chord names.

Chord symbol: **C**   Chord symbol: **G⁷**

Practice changing from the C chord to the G7 chord and back again:

1. The 1st finger plays G in both chords.
2. The 2nd finger plays F in the G7 chord.
3. Only the 5th finger moves out of C Position (down to B) for G7.

🔊 **3-22 (51)**

SOLO REPERTOIRE

🔊 **3-23 (52)**

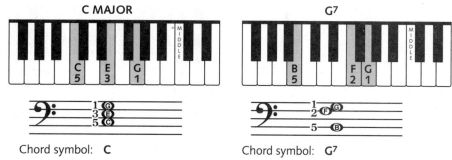

Calypso Tune
arr. by E. L. Lancaster

The F Major Chord

The C major chord is frequently followed by the F major chord, and vice versa.

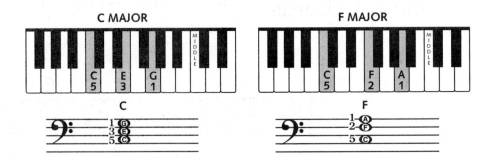

Practice changing from the C chord to the F chord and back again:

1. The 5th finger plays C in both chords.
2. The 2nd finger plays F in the F chord.
3. Only the 1st finger moves out of C Position (up to A) for the F chord.

🔊 3-24 (53)

READING

Simple Gifts

🔊 3-25 (54)

Shaker Hymn

Fermata (⌒)
hold the note longer than its value

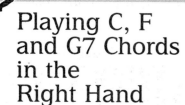

Playing C, F and G7 Chords in the Right Hand

It is very important to be able to play all chords with the *right* hand as well as the *left*. Chords are used in either or both hands in popular and classical music.

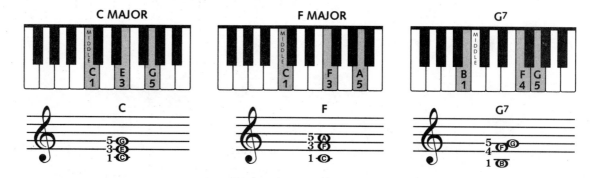

The C, F and G7 chords are built on the 1st, 4th & 5th notes of the C major scale. These three chords are the most important chords in the key and are called **primary chords.**

1. Practice changing from the C chord to the F chord and back again:

   a. The 1st finger plays C in both chords.
   b. The 3rd finger moves up to F.
   c. The 5th finger moves up to A for the F chord.

3-26 (55)

2. Practice changing from the C chord to the G7 chord and back again:

   a. The 5th finger plays G in both chords.
   b. The 4th finger plays F in the G7 chord.
   c. The 1st finger moves out of C Position (down to B) for the G7 chord.

3-27 (56)

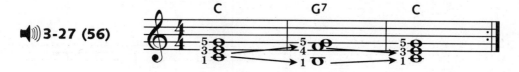

3. Practice the following chord progression that uses primary chords in the key of C major, hands separately.

3-28 (57)

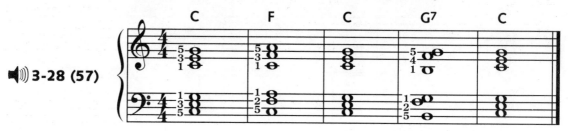

Binary Form (AB)

This piece has two sections (A and B). This overall plan is often called **binary** or **AB form.**

The A section uses scale patterns in the RH and C and G7 chords in the LH.

The B section uses C, F and G7 chords in the RH.

Morning Classic

🔊 3-29 (58)

E. L. Lancaster

Key of G Major

Objectives

Upon completion of this unit the student will be able to:

1. Play the G major scale using traditional fingerings.
2. Identify additional musical concepts (dotted quarter note, finger substitution) and apply them to performance at the keyboard.
3. Build and play the G major, D7 and C major chords in close position in the key of G major.
4. Use the damper pedal in performance.
5. Aurally distinguish C, F and G7 chords in the key of C major, and G, C and D7 chords in the key of G major.

Assignments

Week of _____

Write your assignments for the week in the space below.

_____

_____

_____

_____

_____

_____

_____

_____

_____

_____

Did You Know?

Movies and Music

Many people are introduced to classical music through movies. Since the early days in the motion picture industry, movies have depended on the classics for thematic and background music. Many movies have highlighted music or performers of music, thereby sparking a renewed interest in classical music and its composers and performers. For example, Disney's Fantasia *(1940), which features music by Bach, Schubert, Beethoven, Tchaikovsky and others, earned an Academy Award for widening the scope of the motion picture as entertainment and as an art form.* Amadeus *(1984) chronicles the incredible story of Wolfgang Amadeus Mozart as told by his rival Antonio Salieri. In Mr. Holland's Opus *(1995) Glenn Holland, a musician and composer, is fulfilled as he shares his passion with his high-school music students.* Shine *(1996) traces the life of pianist and child prodigy David Helfgott through emotional trauma and eventually to popular acclaim on the concert stage.*

The G Major Scale

Remember that the major scale is made up of two *tetrachords* joined by a whole step. The second tetrachord of the G major scale begins on D.

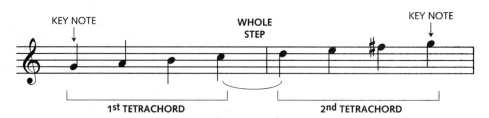

TECHNIQUE

Preparation for Scale Playing

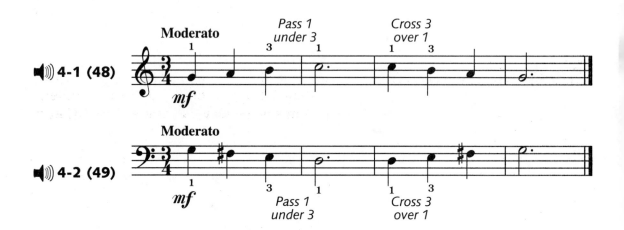

Playing the G Major Scale

A piece based on the G major scale is in the **key of G major.** Since F is sharp in the G scale, every F will be sharp in the key of G major.

Instead of placing a sharp before every F in the entire piece, the sharp is indicated at the beginning in the **key signature.**

Key of G Major
Key Signature: 1 sharp (F♯)
Play all F's sharp throughout

Practice slowly hands separately. Lean the hand slightly in the direction you are moving. The hand should move smoothly along with no twisting motion of the wrist!

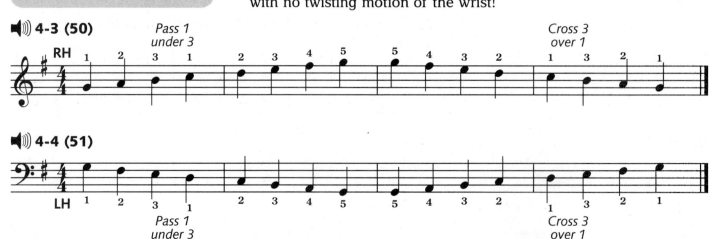

Play the scales above hands together. The RH ascends as the LH descends and vice versa (contrary motion). Both hands play the same numbered fingers at the same time.

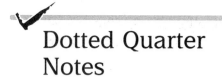

Dotted Quarter Notes

A **dot** increases the length of a note by *one half its value*.

A **dotted half note** is equal to a half note tied to a quarter note.

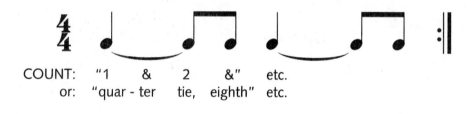

A **dotted quarter note** is equal to a quarter note tied to an eighth note.

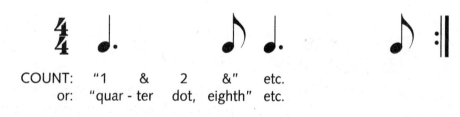

RHYTHM READING

1. Clap (or tap) the following rhythms. Clap once for each note, counting aloud. Notice that the only difference in the two rhythms is the way they are written. They are played the same.

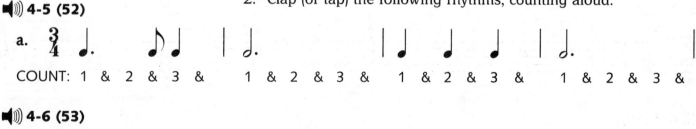

In $\frac{4}{4}$ or $\frac{3}{4}$ time, the dotted quarter note is almost always followed by an eighth note.

2. Clap (or tap) the following rhythms, counting aloud.

4-5 (52)

a.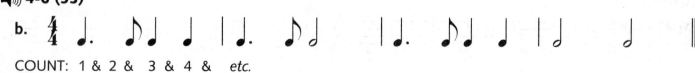

COUNT: 1 & 2 & 3 &   1 & 2 & 3 &   1 & 2 & 3 &   1 & 2 & 3 &

4-6 (53)

b.

COUNT: 1 & 2 & 3 & 4 &   *etc.*

4-7 (54)

c.

COUNT: 1 & 2 & 3 & 4 &   *etc.*

READING

Play the following melodies, counting aloud.

4-8 (55)

Allegro

4-9 (56)

Moderato

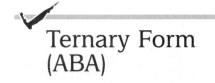

Ternary Form (ABA)

This piece has three sections (A, B, A). This overall plan is often called ternary or ABA form.

SOLO REPERTOIRE

4-10 (57)

Dance

Joachim van der Hofe
(c. 1612)

A Section

Moderato

B Section

A Section

rit. 2nd time

G Major and D7 Chords in the Left Hand

Practice changing from the G chord to the D7 chord and back again:

1. The 1st finger plays D in both chords.
2. The 2nd finger plays C in the D7 chord.
3. Only the 5th finger moves out of G Position (down to F♯) for D7.

🔊 **4-11 (58)**

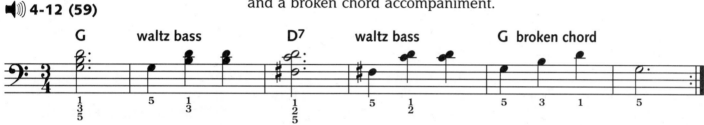

🔊 **4-12 (59)**

The following warm-up introduces a waltz bass accompaniment and a broken chord accompaniment.

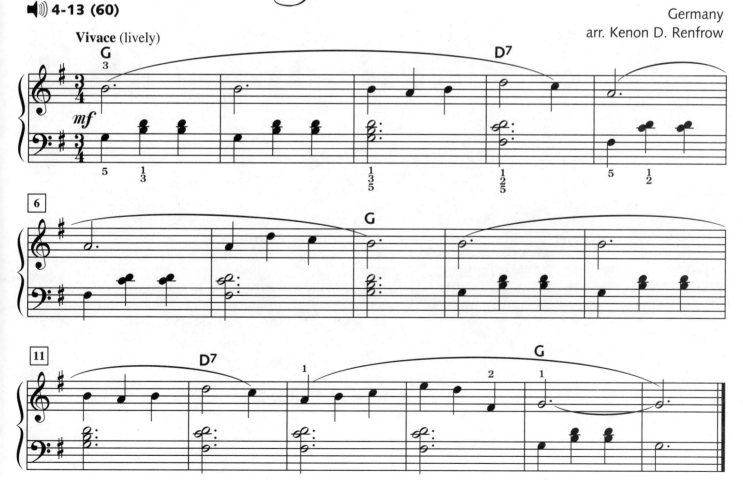

SOLO REPERTOIRE

Du, du liegst mir im Herzen

🔊 **4-13 (60)**

Germany
arr. Kenon D. Renfrow

Vivace (lively)

A New Position of the C Major Chord in the Left Hand

You have already played the C major chord with C as the lowest note: that is **C E G.** When you play these same 3 notes in any order, you still have a C major chord. When you are playing in G position, it is most convenient to play G as the lowest note: **G C E.**

The following diagrams show how easy it is to move from the G major chord to the C major chord, when G is the lowest note of both chords.

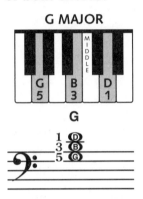

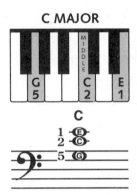

Practice changing from the G chord to the C chord and back again:
1. The 5th finger plays G in both chords.
2. The 2nd finger plays C in the C chord.
3. Only the 1st finger moves out of G Position (up to E) for the C chord.

🔊 **4-14 (61)**

Playing G, C and D7 Chords in the Right Hand

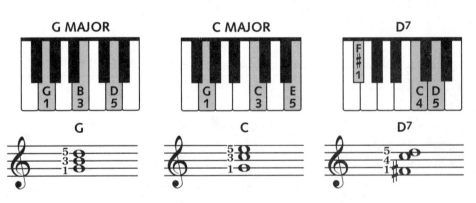

The G, C and D7 chords are built on the 1st, 4th & 5th notes of the G major scale. These three chords are the most important chords in the key and are called **primary chords.**

1. Practice changing from the G chord to the C chord and back again:

a. The 1st finger plays G in both chords.
b. The 3rd finger moves up to C.
c. The 5th finger moves up to E for the C chord.

🔊 **4-15 (62)**

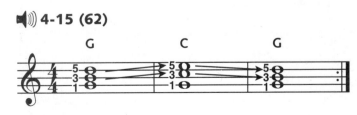

2. Practice changing from the G chord to the D7 chord and back again:

a. The 5th finger plays D in both chords.
b. The 4th plays C in the D7 chord.
c. Only the 1st finger moves out of G Position for the D7 chord.

🔊 **4-16 (63)**

 **4-17 (64)**

3. Practice the following chord progression that uses primary chords in the key of G major, hands separately.

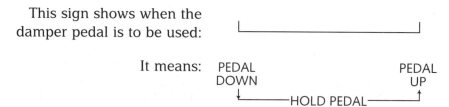

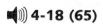

The Damper Pedal

The right pedal is called the **damper pedal.** When you hold the damper pedal down, any tone you play continues after you release the key. The right foot is used on the damper pedal. Always keep your heel on the floor; use your ankle like a hinge.

This sign shows when the damper pedal is to be used:

It means: PEDAL DOWN ↓ ──── HOLD PEDAL ──── ↑ PEDAL UP

The following sign is used to indicate **overlapping pedal.**

At this point, the pedal comes up, and it goes down again immediately!

READING

Pedal Study

 **4-18 (65)**

Moderately slow

mf–p

rit. 2nd time

Kum-Ba-Yah!

🔊 4-19 (66)

Traditional
arr. E. L. Lancaster & Kenon D. Renfrow

*Finger substitution: While holding the key down with finger 4, shift to finger 5.

EAR TRAINING

1. Your teacher will play C, F and G7 chords in the key of C. Circle the chords that you hear.

🔊 4-20 (67)

1a.

🔊 4-21 (68)

1b.

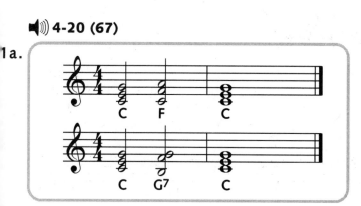

🔊 4-22 (69)

1c.

🔊 4-23 (70)

1d.

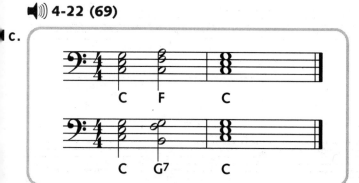 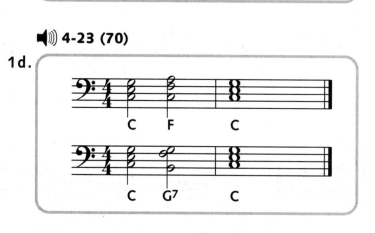

2. Your teacher will play G, C and D7 chords in the key of G. Write the name for each chord on the line. The first chord is shown.

🔊 4-24 (71)

2a. ___G___   _____   _____   _____

🔊 4-25 (72)

2b. ___C___   _____   _____   _____

🔊 4-26 (73)

2c. ___G___   _____   _____   _____

🔊 4-27 (74)

2d. __D7__   _____   _____   _____

Teacher: See page 154.

Review Worksheet

Name _____   Date _____

1. Begin on each given key and build an ascending major five-finger pattern. Write the names of the keys in the blanks.

    G ___ ___ ___ ___

    A ___ ___ ___ ___

    D ___ ___ ___ ___

2. Identify each major five-finger pattern from its black-white key sequence. Write the name of the five-finger pattern in the blank.

    W   W   W   B   W   ___

    W   B   B   W   W   ___

    W   B   B   W   B   ___

3. Identify each chord in the key of C major as C, F or G7 by writing its name on the line.

    ___   ___   ___   ___   ___   ___

4. Identify each chord in the key of G major as G, C or D7 by writing its name on the line.

    ___   ___   ___   ___   ___   ___

5. Draw one note (♩ ♩ or ♪) in each box to complete the measures.

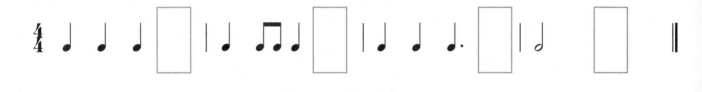

Minor Five-Finger Patterns

Objectives

Upon completion of this unit the student will be able to:

1. Play minor five-finger patterns and triads beginning on any white key.

2. Perform duet repertoire with a partner.

3. Identify additional musical concepts (D.C. al Coda) and apply them to performance at the keyboard.

Assignments

Week of _____

Write your assignments for the week in the space below.

_____

_____

_____

_____

_____

_____

_____

_____

_____

_____

_____

_____

Did You Know?

The Romantic Period

The Romantic period in music history usually refers to the time period from 1820 to 1900. Etudes, concertos, character pieces, dances, and variations were the prevalent music forms. For the first time in music history, the piano was the main keyboard instrument of the period. Romantic music makes use of complex rhythmic patterns and takes musical expression to a higher level through the use of the damper pedal, lyrical melodies, a variety of accompaniment patterns, and numerous tempi and dynamic shadings. Well-known composers from the Romantic period are Frédéric François Chopin, Johannes Brahms, Robert Schumann and Franz Liszt.

Major and Minor Five-Finger Patterns

Major five-finger patterns become minor five-finger patterns when the middle note is lowered a half step.

Major Five-Finger Pattern

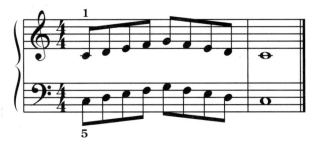

Minor Five-Finger Pattern

Playing Major and Minor Five-Finger Patterns

Play the following exercise that uses major and minor five-finger patterns.

🔊 **4-28 (75)**

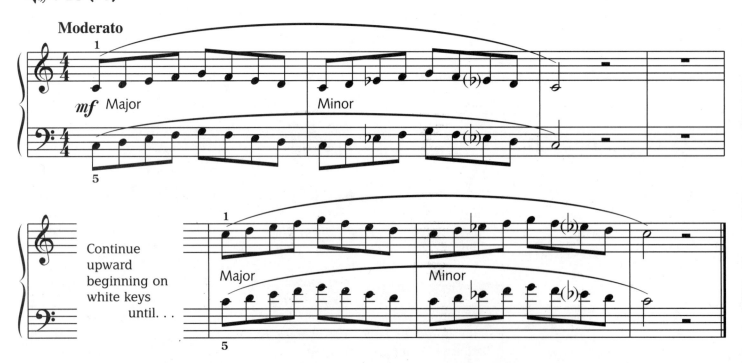

Optional: Play the above exercise beginning on D♭. Continue upward beginning on black keys until the next D♭ is reached.

Minor Chords

Major chords become minor chords when the middle note (3rd) is lowered a half step.

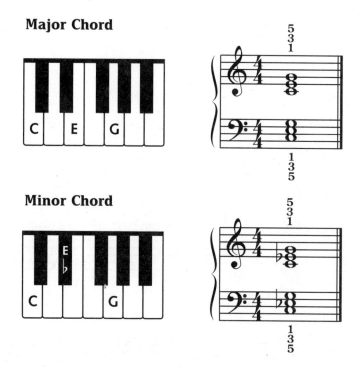

Major Chord

Minor Chord

Playing Minor Five-Finger Patterns and Chords

Play the following exercise that uses minor five-finger patterns and chords.

🔊 **4-29 (76)**

Moderato

mf └ Minor five-finger pattern ┘ └ Broken chord ┘ Block chord

Continue upward beginning on white keys until. . .

DUET: SECONDO

Teacher

Galop

from *The Children's Musical Friend*

🔊 4-30 (77)

Heinrich Wohlfahrt (1797–1883)
Op. 87, No. 15

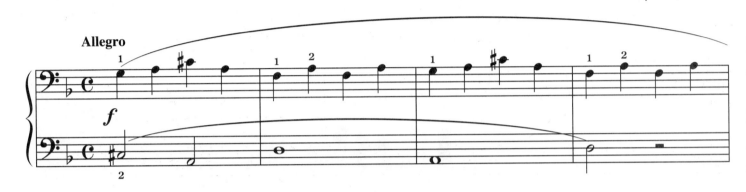

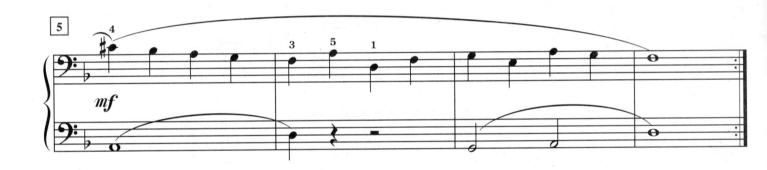

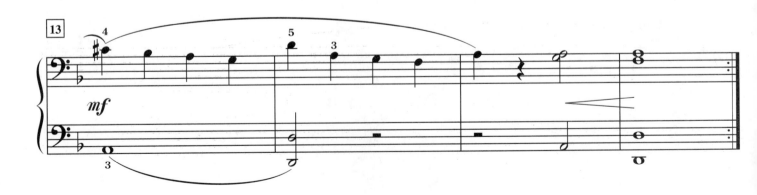

Student

Galop

from *The Children's Musical Friend*

🔊 4-30 (77)

Heinrich Wohlfahrt (1797–1883)

Op. 87, No. 15

Allegro

(Both hands one octave higher than written throughout)

Master Mind

🔊 **4-31 (78)**

E. L. Lancaster

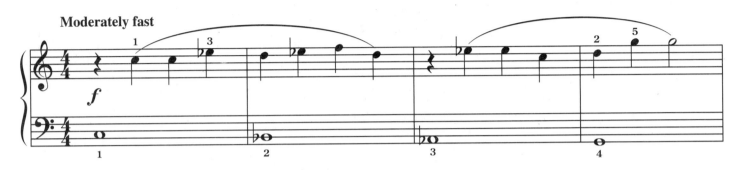

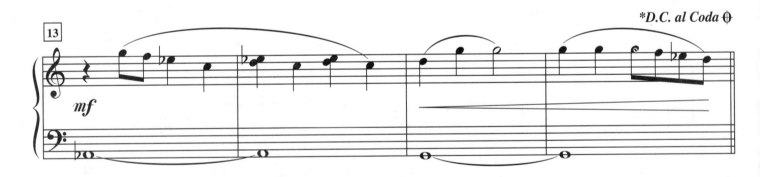

* **D. C. (da capo) al Coda**
means repeat from the
beginning to the ⊕, then
skip to the **Coda**
(an added ending).

** Suddenly

Triads and Arpeggios

Objectives

Upon completion of this unit the student will be able to:

1. Expand the reading range by playing repertoire using notes surrounding five C's.
2. Play triads of the keys of C major and G major.
3. Play major and minor hand-over-hand arpeggios beginning on white keys.
4. Aurally distinguish rhythm patterns.
5. Harmonize a melody from a lead sheet using major chords with block chord and broken chord accompaniment patterns.

Assignments

Week of _____

Write your assignments for the week in the space below.

_____

_____

_____

_____

_____

_____

_____

_____

_____

_____

_____

_____

_____

Did You Know?

Frédéric François Chopin

*F*rédéric François Chopin (1810–1849) remains one of the greatest composers of piano music of all time. Chopin, like Mozart, showed signs of great musical promise as a young child. He was born in Warsaw, Poland, to a Polish mother and French father. Although aware of his natural ability, his family insisted on a thorough education. He wrote nearly 250 compositions for piano and achieved for it a new height of expression and nuance. Franz Liszt called Chopin "a poet—elegiac, profound, chaste, and dreaming." Although he spent much of his adult life in Paris, he remained a fiercely patriotic Pole. This patriotism is reflected in both his mazurkas and polonaises (Polish dances). He died from tuberculosis at the age of 39.

Five C's

Five C's provide valuable reference points for reading music.

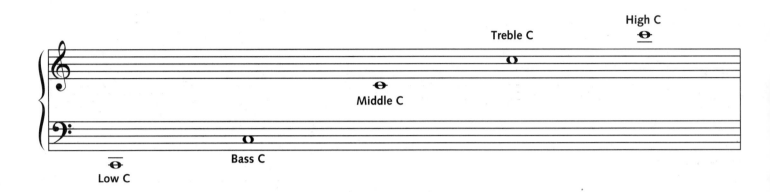

Play the following exercise that uses the five C positions.

◀))) **4-32 (79)**

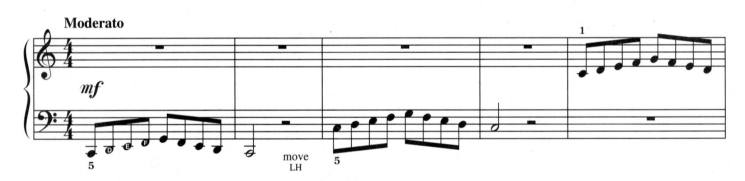

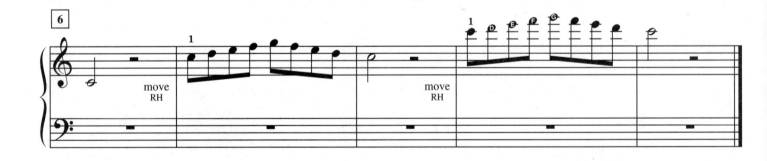

Playing Triads of the Key

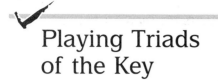

Triads may be built on any note of any scale. The sharps or flats in the key signature must be used when playing these triads.

Play triads of the key in C major.

◀))) **4-33 (80)**

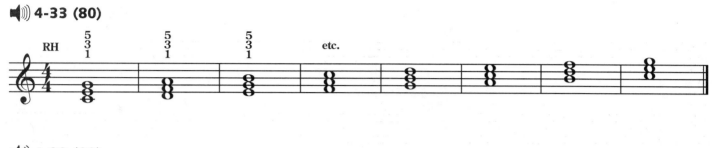

◀))) **4-33 (80)**

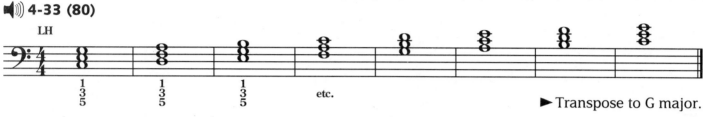

▶ Transpose to G major.

(Remember: The key of G major has one sharp—F♯.)

Playing Major Chords (Hand-over-Hand)

Play the following exercise that uses major chords.

◀))) **4-34 (81)**

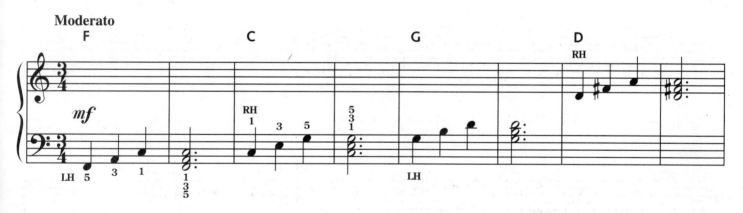

Optional: Play the above exercise, changing each chord to minor by lowering the middle note a half step.

Parallel Moves

🔊 4-35 (82)

Kenon D. Renfrow

Moderately fast

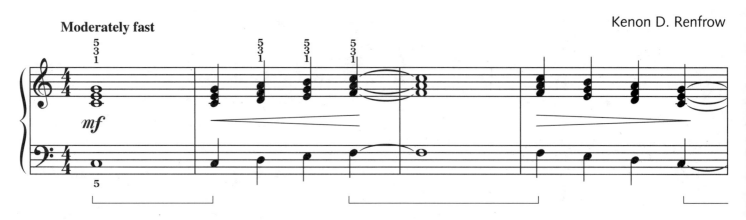

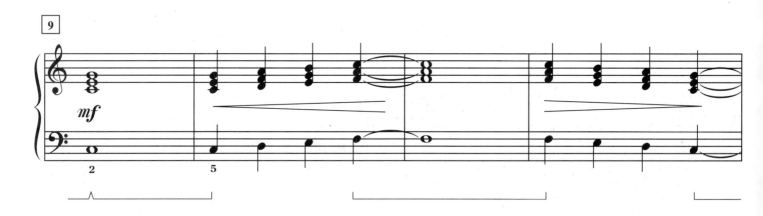

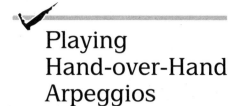

Playing Hand-over-Hand Arpeggios

An **arpeggio** is a broken chord; pitches are sounded successively rather than simultaneously.

Play the following major and minor hand-over-hand arpeggios.

🔊 **4-36 (83)**

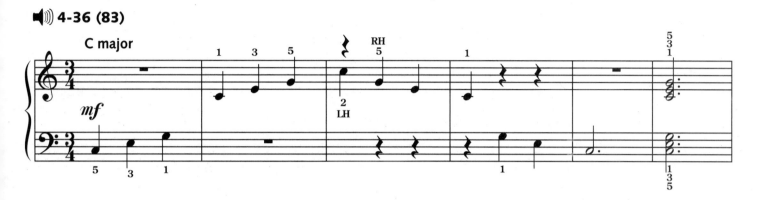

Continue upward beginning on white keys until. . .

A New Day

🔊 **4-37 (84)**

E. L. Lancaster

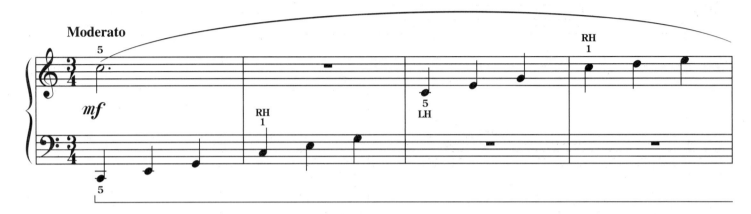

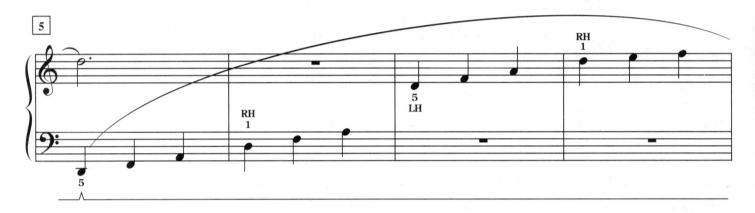

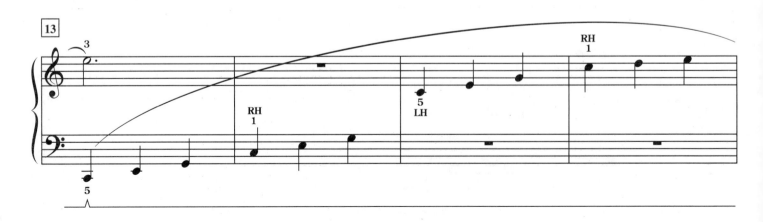

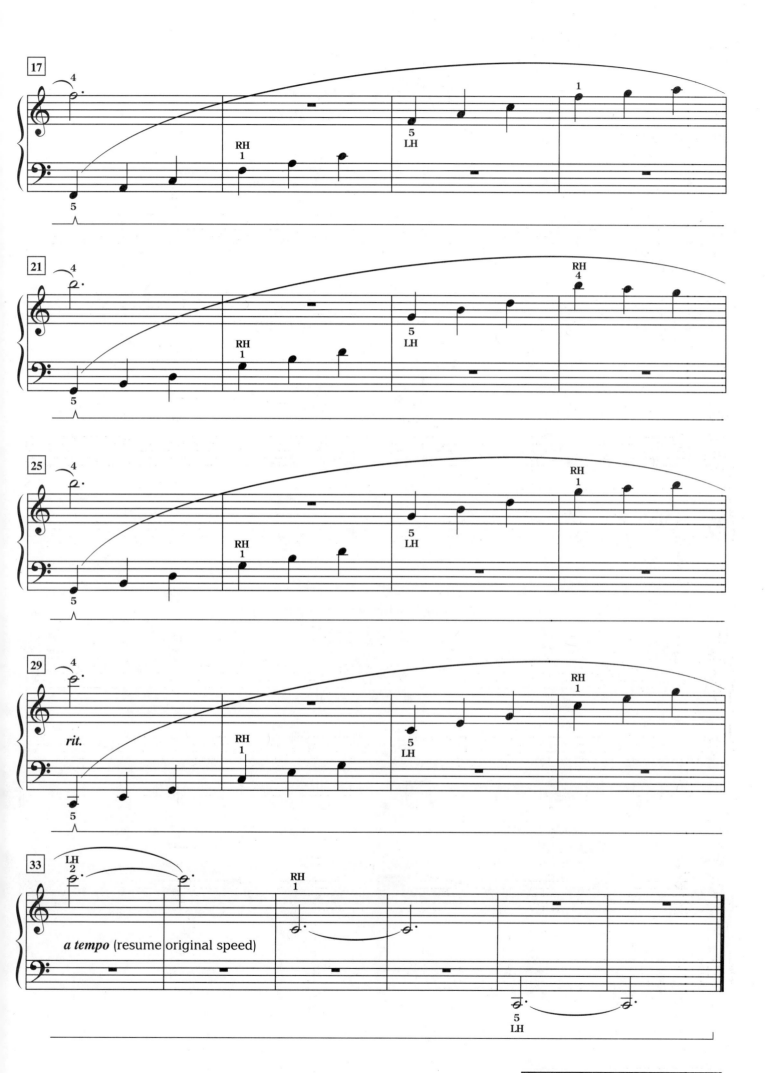

EAR TRAINING

1. Your teacher will clap a rhythm pattern.
   Circle the pattern that you hear.

2. Your teacher will clap a rhythm pattern.
   Add a curved line for each tie that you hear.

🔊 4-42 (89)

2a.

🔊 4-43 (90)

2b.

🔊 4-44 (91)

2c.

🔊 4-45 (92)

2d.

Teacher: See page 154.

Harmonizing Melodies from a Lead Sheet

Many pianists find it enjoyable and rewarding to be able to add left-hand parts to right-hand melodies. This process is called **harmonizing** the melody. The most common format for music of this type is the **lead sheet.** The lead sheet gives the melody on a single staff with chord names written above the staff. Since only the melody of these tunes is notated, you must be able to play the chords indicated above the staff in the left hand while playing the melody in the right hand.

The ability to play from a lead sheet opens countless possibilities for repertoire that otherwise may be unavailable or too difficult to play in its original form.

For example, almost any tune imaginable can be found in a "fake book." Fake books are collections that contain a wide variety of melodies in lead sheet format.

In measures where no chords are indicated, the last chord from the previous measure is repeated on beat one. As you work to develop these skills, you will want to alter the left-hand accompaniment style as you play.

1. Using the indicated chords, harmonize the following melody by continuing the block-chord accompaniment pattern given in the first two measures.

Wooden Heart

Germany

2. Using the indicated chords, harmonize the same melody by continuing the broken-chord accompaniment pattern given in the first two measures.

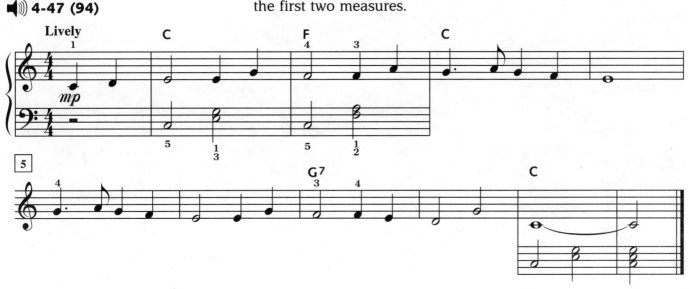

6ths, 7ths and 8ths (Octaves)

Objectives

Upon completion of this unit the student will be able to:

1. Identify melodic and harmonic intervals of 6ths, 7ths and 8ths (octaves) in the keys of C major and G major on the staff and perform them on the keyboard.

2. Perform solo repertoire that uses 6ths, 7ths and 8ths (octaves).

3. Aurally distinguish intervals of 6ths, 7ths and 8ths (octaves) in the key of C major.

4. Harmonize a melody from a lead sheet using major and minor chords with block chord and broken chord accompaniment patterns.

Assignments

Week of _____

Write your assignments for the week in the space below.

_____

_____

_____

_____

_____

_____

_____

_____

_____

_____

_____

_____

Did You Know?

The Piano Concerto

The piano concerto is a work for orchestra that highlights the piano as a solo instrument. Although Mozart highly refined the form, several other composers, among them Beethoven, Brahms and Rachmaninoff, also composed monumental piano concertos. The piano concerto often is presented in three distinct movements, usually fast-slow-fast. Frequently, a cadenza appears near the end of the first and/or last movements. The cadenza provides the opportunity for the performer to improvise on the thematic material already presented in the movement and to display a high degree of virtuosity. Piano concertos continue to be written and performed in this century.

6ths

When you skip four white keys, the interval is a 6th.
6ths are written line-space or space-line.

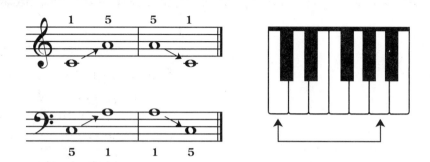

Play the following exercises that use intervals.
Transpose each example to G major.

 5-1 (43)

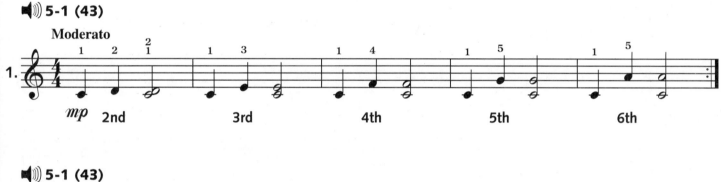

1.

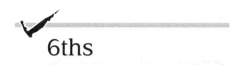 5-1 (43)

2.

 5-2 (44)

3.

 5-2 (44)

4.

Optional: Play exercises 1 and 2 hands together,
and exercises 3 and 4 hands together.

Waltzing in Sixths

🔊 **5-3 (45)**

E. L. Lancaster

Slow waltz tempo

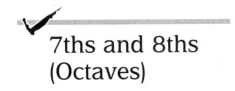

7ths and 8ths (Octaves)

When you skip five white keys, the interval is a 7th.
7ths are written line-line or space-space.

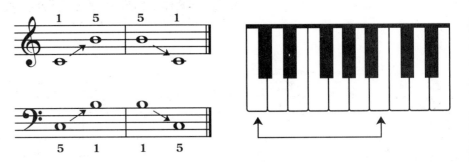

When you skip six white keys, the interval is an 8th (octave).
Octaves are written line-space or space-line.

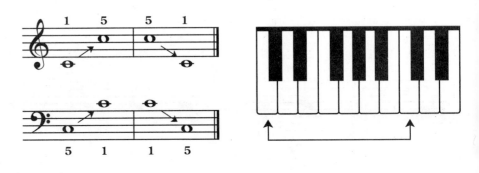

Playing Intervals

Play the following exercises that use intervals.
Transpose each example to G major.

 5-4 (46)

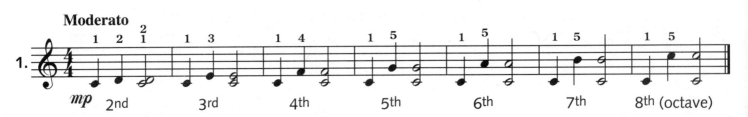

1. Moderato
   mp 2nd 3rd 4th 5th 6th 7th 8th (octave)

 5-4 (46)

2. Moderato
   mp 2nd 3rd 4th 5th 6th 7th 8th (octave)

Optional: Play exercises 1 and 2 hands together.

Summer Memories

E. L. Lancaster
and Kenon D. Renfrow

5-5 (47)

EAR TRAINING

1. Your teacher will play intervals of a 6th or 7th.
   Circle the interval that you hear.

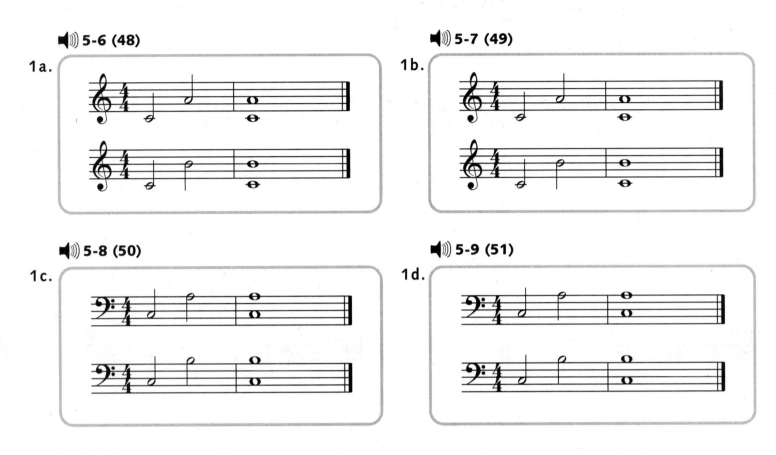

2. Your teacher will play intervals of a 7th or an octave (8th).
   Circle the interval that you hear.

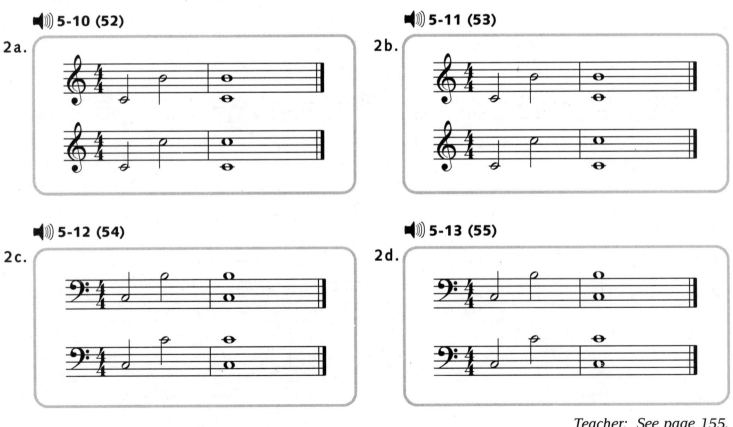

Teacher: See page 155.

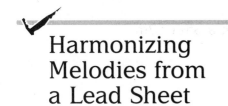

Harmonizing Melodies from a Lead Sheet

Using the indicated chords, harmonize the following melody by continuing the waltz-style accompaniment pattern given in measure 1. Use root position triads except where other positions are suggested.

Meet Me in St. Louis, Louis

🔊 5-14 (56)

Kerry Mills
(1869–1948)

Review Worksheet

Name _____   Date _____

1. Write letter names on the correct keys to form each minor five-finger pattern.

Example

C Minor

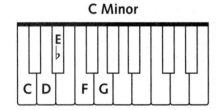

D Minor

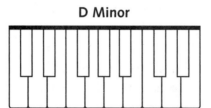

G Minor

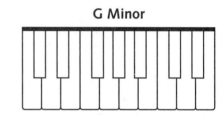

E Minor

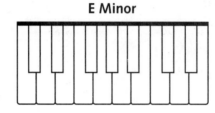

A Minor

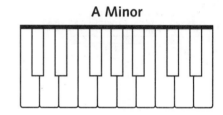

F Minor

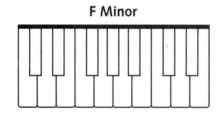

B Minor

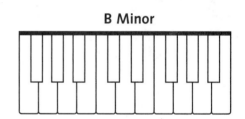

2. In each measure below, draw a whole note above the given note to make the indicated harmonic interval.

7th   6th   8th (octave)   7th   8th (octave)   7th   7th   6th

3. Identify each note by writing its name on the line.

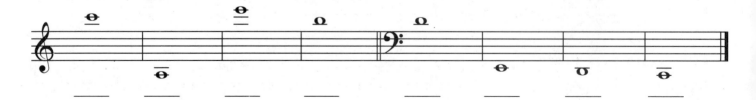

____   ____   ____   ____   ____   ____   ____   ____

The Key of F Major

Objectives

Upon completion of this unit the student will be able to:

1. Expand the reading range by playing repertoire that uses notes surrounding four F's.
2. Play the F major scale using traditional fingerings.
3. Build and play the F major, C7 and B♭ major chords in close position in the key of F major.
4. Perform solo repertoire that uses primary chords in the key of F major.
5. Aurally distinguish I, IV and V7 chords in the key of F major.
6. Harmonize a melody from a lead sheet, using major chords with block chord and waltz bass accompaniment patterns.
7. Perform ensemble repertoire with partners.

Assignments

Week of _____

Write your assignments for the week in the space below.

_____

_____

_____

_____

_____

_____

_____

_____

_____

_____

_____

Did You Know?

The Contemporary Period

The Contemporary period in music history is the period in which we now live. This term is used to refer to music composed from around 1900 to the present. Character pieces, dances, preludes, toccatas, variations, and aleatoric (chance) music are the prevalent forms of serious music, while jazz, ragtime and other popular musical styles have emerged as truly American idioms. Dissonance, prepared instruments and 20th-century notation combine to create a variety of new sounds. The piano continues to be the principal keyboard instrument for serious music styles; however, electronic keyboards, digital pianos and synthesizers are used extensively in popular styles. Well-known composers from the Contemporary period are Béla Bartók, John Cage, Aaron Copland, George Gershwin, Scott Joplin, Dmitri Kabalevsky and Sergei Prokofiev.

Four F's

Four F's provide valuable reference points for reading music.

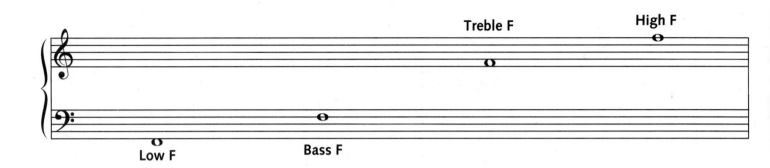

Treble F **High F**

Low F **Bass F**

Play the following exercise that uses the four F positions.

◀))) **5-15 (57)**

Moderato

mf

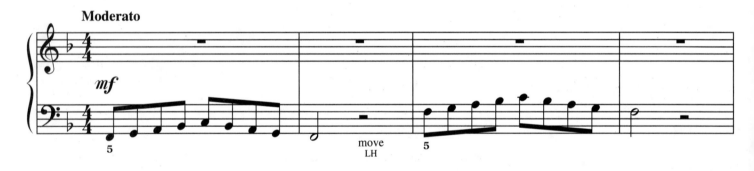

5

move
LH

5

5

1

move
RH

1

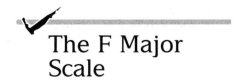

The F Major Scale

Remember that the major scale is made up of two **tetrachords** joined by a whole step. The second tetrachord of the F major scale begins on C.

There is one flat (B♭) in the F major scale.

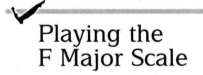

Preparation for Scale Playing

🔊 **5-16 (58)**

🔊 **5-17 (59)**

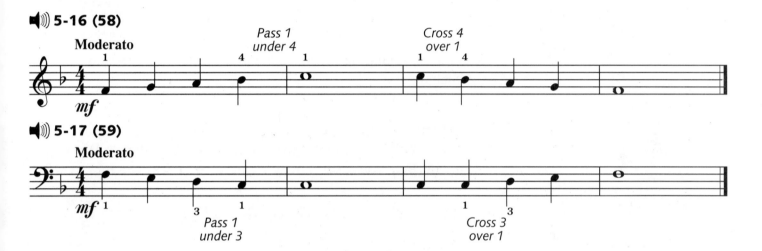

Playing the F Major Scale

A piece based on the F major scale is in the **key of F major.** Since B is flat in the F scale, every B will be flat in the key of F major.

Instead of placing a flat before every B in the entire piece, the flat is indicated at the beginning in the **key signature.**

Practice slowly hands separately. Lean the hand slightly in the direction you are moving. The hand should move smoothly along with no twisting motion of the wrist!

To play the F major scale with the RH, the 5th finger is not used! The fingers fall in the following groups:
1 2 3 4 – 1 2 3 4 ascending; 4 3 2 1 – 4 3 2 1 descending.

Key of F Major
Key Signature: 1 flat (B♭)

🔊 **5-18 (60)**

🔊 **5-18 (60)**

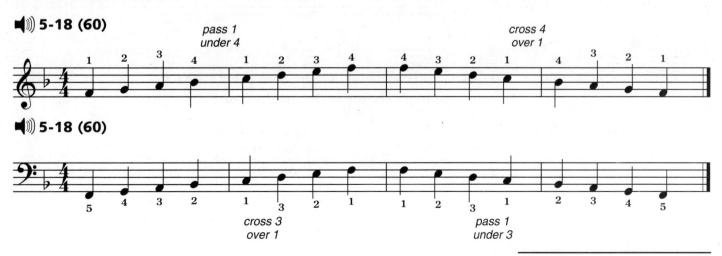

Playing F, B♭ and C7 Chords in the Left Hand

The F, B♭ and C7 chords are built on the 1st, 4th & 5th notes of the F major scale. These three chords are the most important chords in the key and are called **primary chords.**

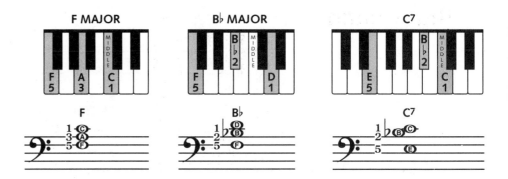

1. Practice changing from the F chord to the B♭ chord and back again:

   a. The 5th finger plays F in both chords.
   b. The 2nd finger plays B♭ in the B♭ chord.
   c. Only the 1st finger moves out of F position (up to D) for the B♭ chord.

🔊 5-19 (61)

2. Practice changing from the F chord to the C7 chord and back again:

   a. The 1st finger plays C in both chords.
   b. The 2nd finger plays B♭ in the C7 chord.
   c. The 5th finger moves out of F position (down to E) for the C7 chord.

🔊 5-20 (62)

3. Practice the following chord progression that uses primary chords in the key of F major.

🔊 5-21 (63)

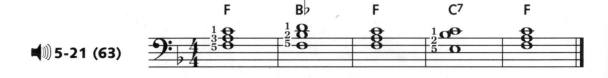

Playing F, B♭ and C7 Chords in the Right Hand

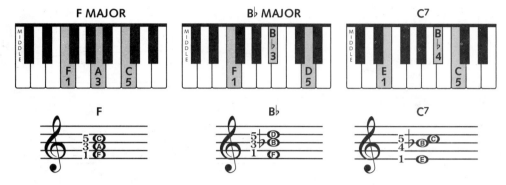

1. Practice changing from the F chord to the B♭ chord and back again:

   a. The 1st finger plays F in both chords.
   b. The 3rd finger movers up to B♭.
   c. The 5th finger moves up to D for the B♭ chord.

   🔊 5-22 (64)

   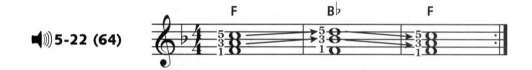

2. Practice changing from the F chord to the C7 chord and back again:

   a. The 5th finger plays C in both chords.
   b. The 4th finger plays B♭ in the C7 chord.
   c. The 1st finger moves out of F position (down to E) for the C7 chord.

   🔊 5-23 (65)

   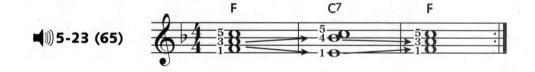

3. Practice the following chord progression that uses primary chords in the key of F major.

   🔊 5-24 (66)

   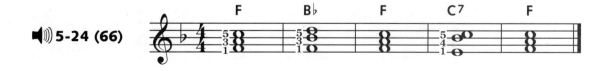

Michael, Row the Boat Ashore

(Chords in LH)

🔊 5-25 (67)

United States

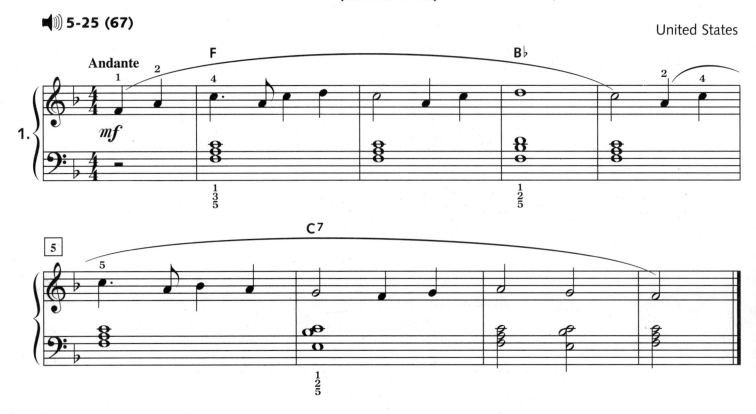

Michael, Row the Boat Ashore

(Chords in RH)

🔊 5-26 (68)

United States

A Classic Tale

◀)) 5-27 (69)

E. L. Lancaster

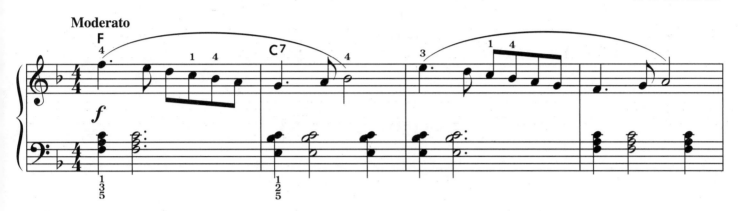

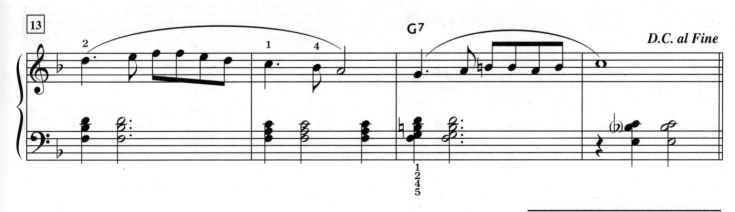

EAR TRAINING

1. Your teacher will play F, B♭ and C7 chords in the key of F.
   Write the name for each chord on the line. The first chord
   is shown.

   🔊 **5-28 (70)**   a.   <u>F</u>   ____   ____   ____

   🔊 **5-29 (71)**   b.   <u>F</u>   ____   ____   ____

   🔊 **5-30 (72)**   c.   <u>C7</u>   ____   ____   ____

   🔊 **5-31 (73)**   d.   <u>B♭</u>   ____   ____   ____

2. Your teacher will play a *block* chord followed by a *broken* chord.
   Write the notes of the *broken* chord in the order they are
   played, using quarter notes.

   🔊 **5-32 (74)**   a.

   🔊 **5-33 (75)**   b.

   🔊 **5-34 (76)**   c.

   🔊 **5-35 (77)**   d.

Teacher: See page 155.

Harmonizing Melodies from a Lead Sheet

1. Using the indicated chords, harmonize the following melody by continuing the block-chord accompaniment pattern given in the first two measures.

Dona Nobis Pacem

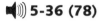 5-36 (78)

Anonymous

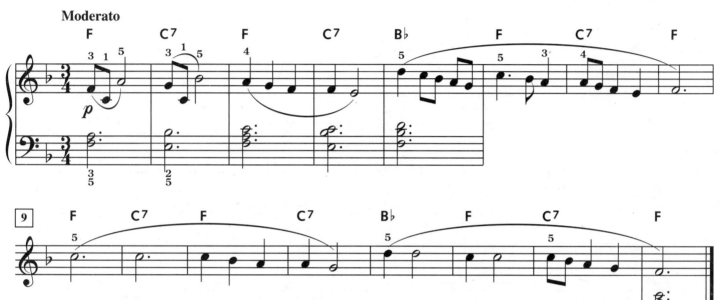

2. Using the indicated chords, harmonize the same melody by continuing the waltz-bass accompaniment pattern given in the first two measures.

 5-37 (79)

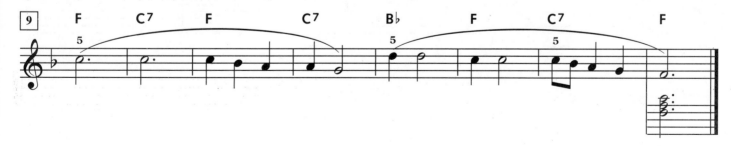

Barcarolle

5-38 (80)

E. L. Lancaster

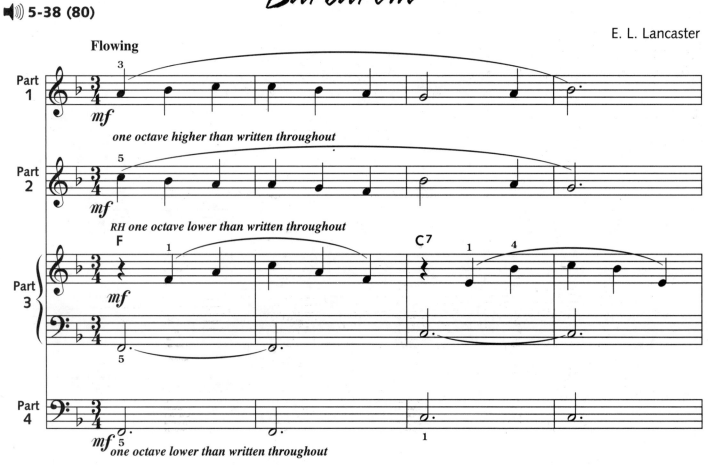

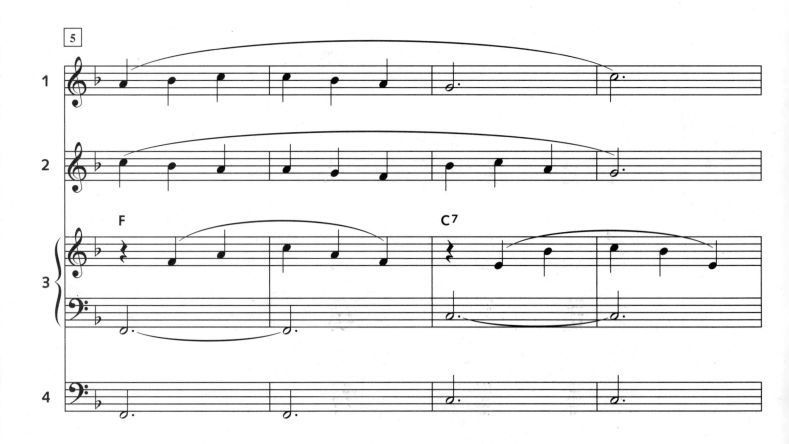

12-Bar Blues

Objectives

Upon completion of this unit the student will be able to:

1. Play five-finger blues patterns in C, G and F over the 12-bar blues chord progression.
2. Identify additional musical concepts (cut time, molto, subito) and apply them to performance at the keyboard.

Assignments

Week of _____

Write your assignments for the week in the space below.

_____

_____

_____

_____

_____

_____

_____

_____

_____

_____

_____

_____

_____

_____

_____

_____

_____

Did You Know?

George Gershwin

George Gershwin (1898–1937), the son of Russian immigrants, grew up in humble surroundings in Brooklyn, New York. As a teenager, he was hired to "plug" songs on Tin Pan Alley for the Remick Publishing Company. His first great hit song was "Swanee." He often worked with his brother Ira, who wrote lyrics for many of his songs and musicals. Subsequently, he wrote songs for Hollywood films, an opera Porgy and Bess, and concert pieces such as "Rhapsody in Blue." He is remembered as one of the first composers to successfully fuse jazz and classical music. He died in 1937 of a brain tumor at the age of 39.

12-Bar Blues

The blues follows a strict 12-bar pattern. Using block chords, play the 12-bar blues pattern with the left hand.

This five-finger blues pattern may be used to create melodies over the blues chord progression. Play the five-finger blues pattern in C, G and F.

READING

🔊 **5-39 (81)**

*Optional: The eighth notes may be played a bit unevenly: long short long short, *etc.*

Sixth Street Boogie

🔊 5-40 (82)

*Optional: The eighth notes may be played a bit unevenly: long   short   long   short, *etc.*

A Little Blues

🔊 5-41 (83)

Gayle Kowalchyk
E. L. Lancaster

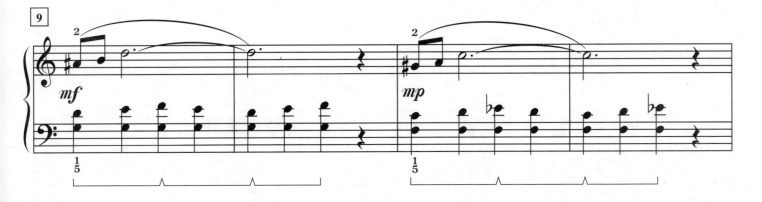

"A Little Blues" from BOOGIE 'N' BLUES, Book 2, by Gayle Kowalchyk and E. L. Lancaster
Copyright © MCMXCIII by Alfred Publishing Co., Inc.

New Time Signature

¢ This time signature is **alla breve**, sometimes called "cut time." This indicates $\frac{2}{2}$ time. Count *one* for each half note, etc.

SOLO REPERTOIRE

Toccatina

🔊 **5-42 (84)**

E. L. Lancaster

"Toccatina" from ALFRED'S GROUP PIANO FOR ADULTS, Book 1, by E. L. Lancaster and Kenon D. Renfrow
Copyright © MCMXCV by Alfred Publishing Co., Inc.

Review Worksheet

Name _____   Date _____

1. Identify each major scale below by writing its name on the indicated line. Write the correct RH fingering on the line above the staff
   and the correct LH fingering on the line below the staff.

_____ major

_____ major

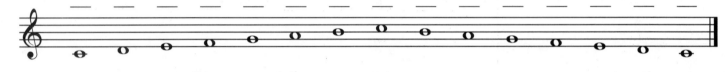

_____ major

2. Identify each chord in the key of C major as
   C, F or G7 by writing its name on the line.

3. Identify each chord in the key of F major as
   F, B♭ or C7 by writing its name on the line.

4. Identify each chord in the key of G major as
   G, C or D7 by writing its name on the line.

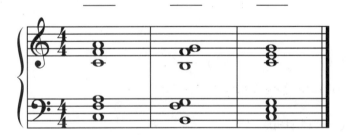

5. Write the numbers from column A in the appropriate blanks
   in column B to match each item with its best description.

Column A	Column B
1. Natural sign ♮	_____ Moderately loud
2. A tempo	_____ Play next key to the right
3. Repeat sign :‖	_____ Suddenly
4. Molto	_____ Smoothly connected
5. Crescendo	_____ Very short
6. Phrase	_____ Locates the G above the middle of the keyboard
7. Subito	_____ ▬
8. Sharp sign ♯	_____ Locates the F below the middle of the keyboard
9. Flat sign ♭	_____ Gradually louder
10. Ritardando	_____ Loud
11. Mezzo forte *mf*	_____ 3 beats in a measure, quarter note gets 1 beat
12. Whole step	_____ A musical thought or sentence
13. Treble clef sign 𝄞	_____ Gradually softer
14. Bass clef sign 𝄢	_____ Play next key to the left
15. Piano *p*	_____ ξ
16. Diminuendo	_____ Much
17. ¾	_____ ▬
18. 4/4	_____ Repeat from the beginning
19. Forte *f*	_____ Equals two half steps
20. Legato	_____ Soft
21. Staccato	_____ Cancels a sharp or flat
22. Quarter rest ‧	_____ Gradually slowing
23. Half rest	_____ Resume original tempo
24. Whole rest	_____ 4 beats in a measure, quarter note gets 1 beat

Give My Regards to Broadway

🔊 **6-1 (12)**

George M. Cohan (1878–1942)
arr. by E. L. Lancaster & Kenon D. Renfrow

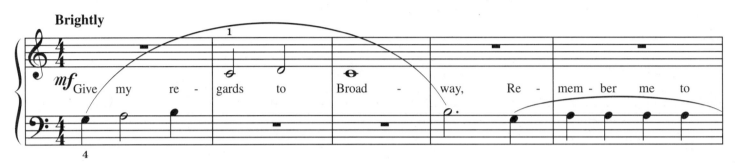

Give my re - gards to Broad - way, Re - mem - ber me to

TEACHER ACCOMPANIMENT (Student plays 1 octave higher.)

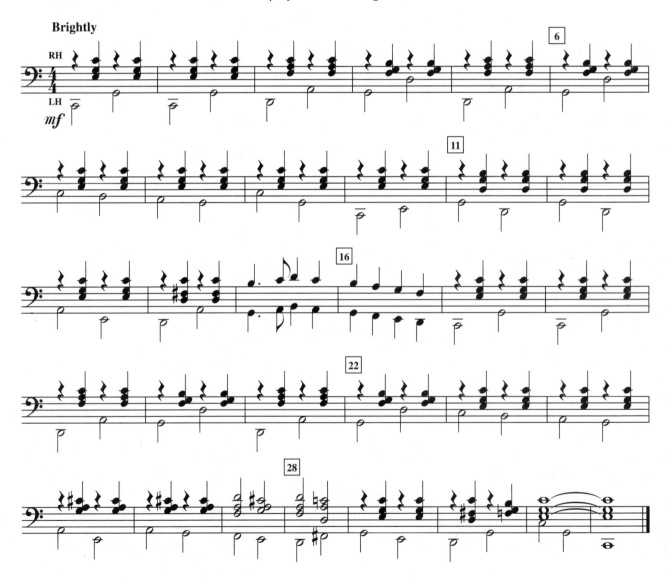

You're a Grand Old Flag

6-2 (13)

George M. Cohan (1878–1942)
arr. by Gayle Kowalchyk & E. L. Lancaster

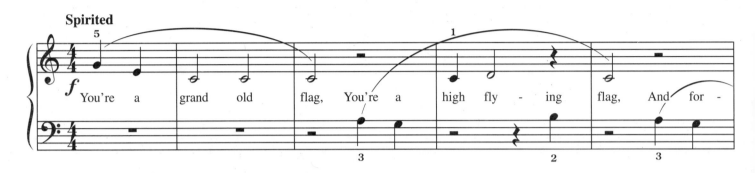

Spirited

You're a grand old flag, You're a high fly - ing flag, And for -

TEACHER ACCOMPANIMENT (Student plays 1 octave higher.)

Spirited

"You're a Grand Old Flag" from PATRIOTIC FESTIVAL by Gayle Kowalchyk and E. L. Lancaster
Copyright © MCMXCI by Alfred Publishing Co., Inc.

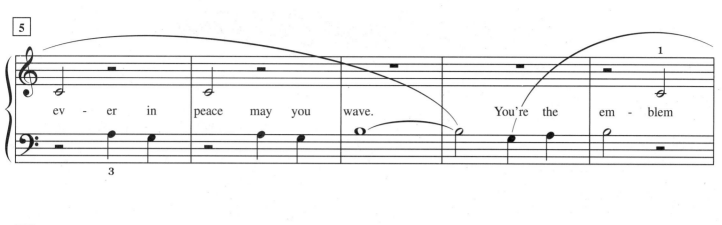

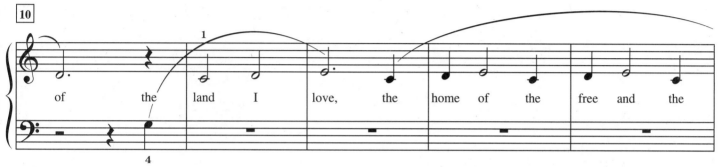

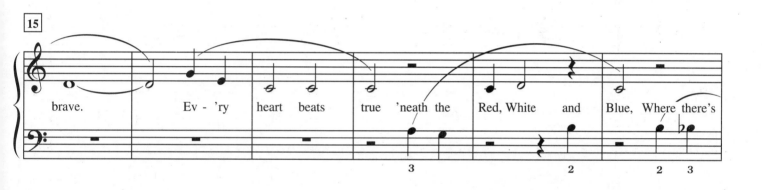

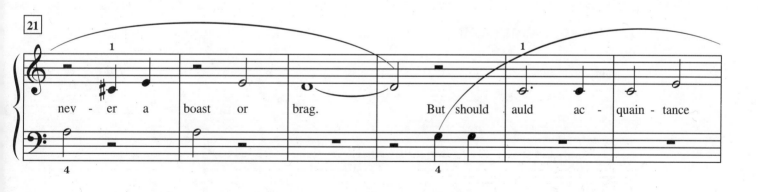

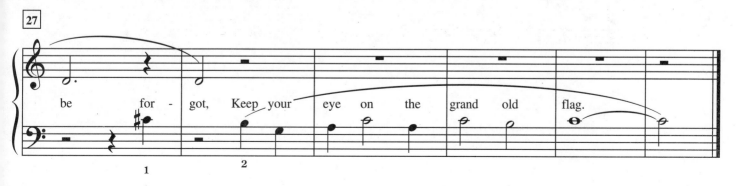

Amazing Grace

United States
arr. by E. L. Lancaster
& Kenon D. Renfrow

6-3 (14)

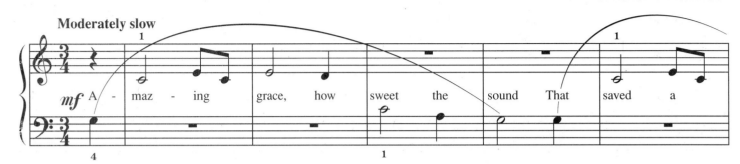

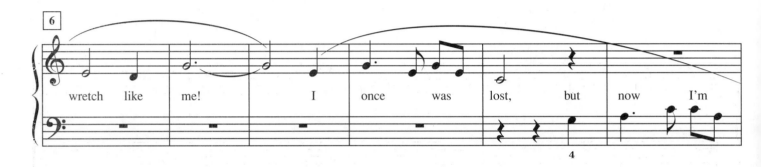

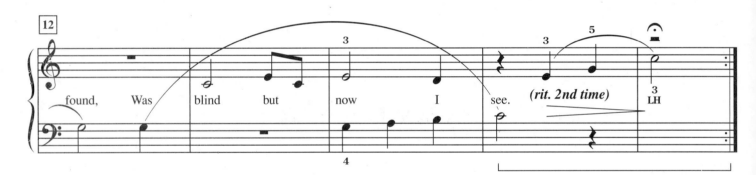

TEACHER ACCOMPANIMENT (Student plays 1 octave higher.)

March No. 1

🔊 6-4 (15)

Daniel Gottlob Türk
(1756–1813)

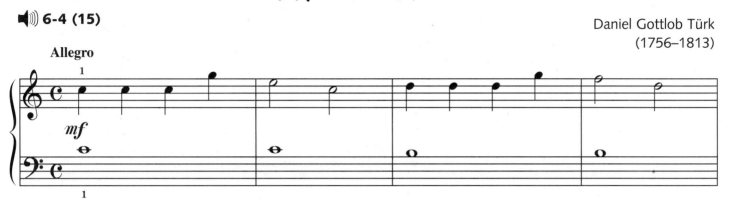

March No. 2

🔊 6-5 (16)

Daniel Gottlob Türk
(1756–1813)

Vivace

Cornelius Gurlitt (1820–1901)
Op. 117, No. 8

🔊 6-6 (17)

Canon

Johann Pachelbel (1653–1706)
arr. Kenon D. Renfrow

6-7 (18)

Moderato

simile (continue pedal in the same manner)

Für Elise

Ludwig van Beethoven (1770–1827)
arr. by E. L. Lancaster & Kenon D. Renfrow

6-8 (19)

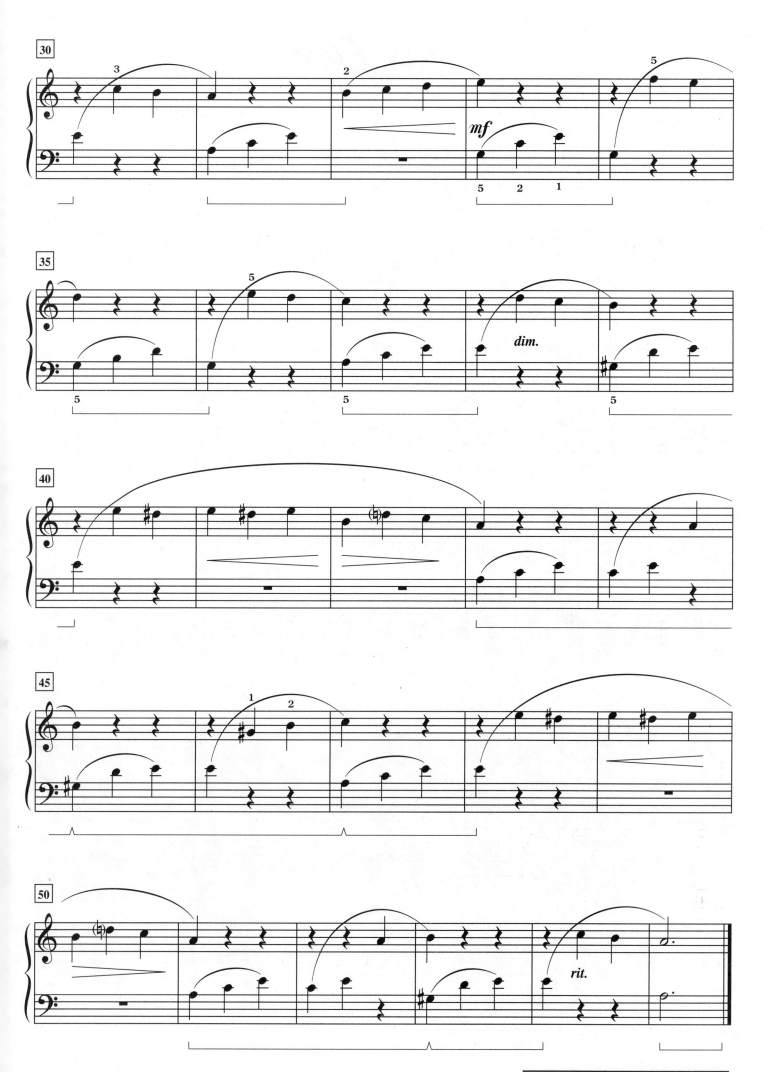

Jingle Bells

🔊 6-9 (20)

James Pierpont (1822–1893)
arr. by Gayle Kowalchyk & E. L. Lancaster

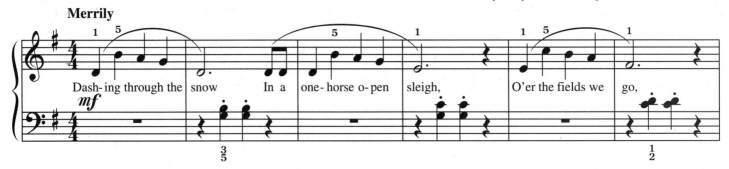

Dash-ing through the snow   In a one-horse o-pen sleigh,   O'er the fields we go,

TEACHER ACCOMPANIMENT (Student plays 1 octave higher.)

"Jingle Bells" from CHRISTMAS FESTIVAL, Book 2, by Gayle Kowalchyk and E. L. Lancaster
Copyright © MCMXCI by Alfred Publishing Co., Inc.

Celebration Boogie

Gayle Kowalchyk
E. L. Lancaster

*Optional: The eighth notes may be played a bit unevenly: long   short   long   short, *etc.*

"Celebration Boogie" from BOOGIE 'N' BLUES, Book 2 by Gayle Kowalchyk and E. L. Lancaster
Copyright © MCMXCIII by Alfred Publishing Co., Inc.

Jacob's Ladder

Spiritual
arr. by Kenon D. Renfrow

Appendix A

Page 17 (Play)

Page 48 (Play)

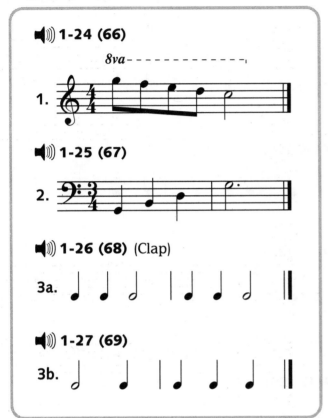

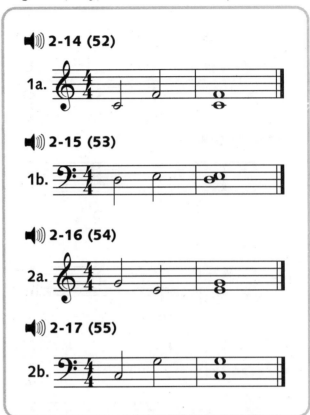

Page 65 (Play)

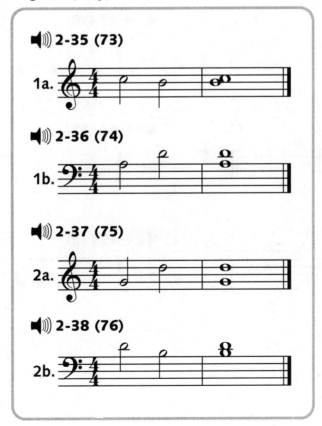

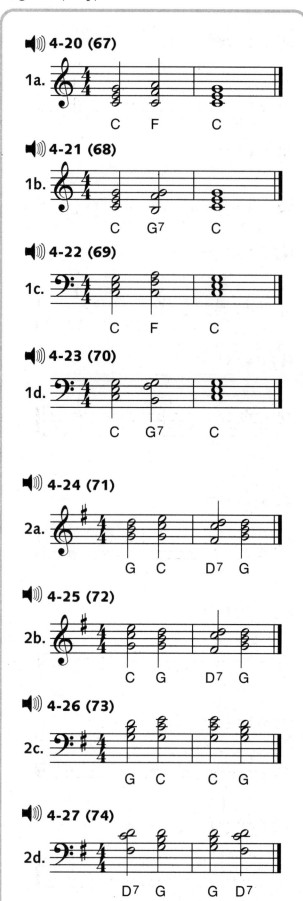

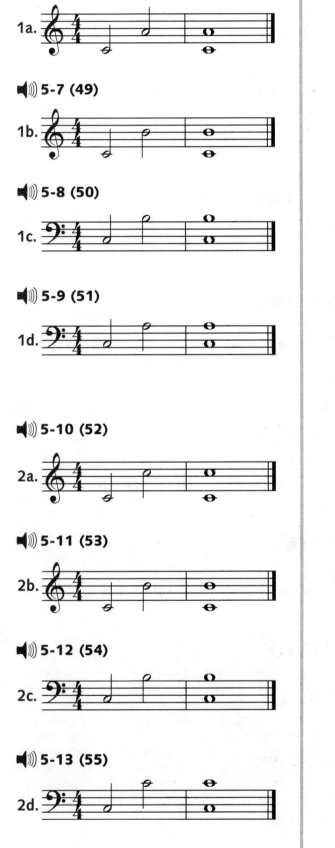

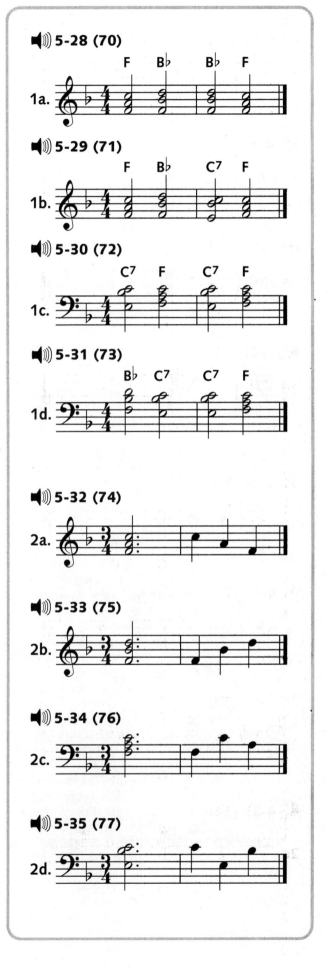

Appendix B

Accent sign (>) . . . placed over or under a note that gets special emphasis; play that note louder.

Adagio . . . . slowly.

Alla breve (¢) . . . . cut time or $\frac{2}{2}$ time.

Allegretto . . . . . . moderately fast.

Allegro . . . . quickly, happily.

Andante . . . . . . moving along (the word actually means "walking").

Arpeggio . . . . . . broken chord; pitches are sounded successively rather than simultaneously.

A tempo . . . . resume original speed.

Binary form (AB) . . a piece divided into two sections: A and B.

Chromatic scale . . . made up entirely of half steps; it goes up and down, using every key, black and white.

Coda . . . . an added ending.

Coda sign (⊕) . . . . indication to proceed to coda.

Common time (C) . . same as $\frac{4}{4}$ time.

Crescendo (<) . . . gradually louder.

Cut time (¢) . . . . . same as $\frac{2}{2}$ time; alla breve.

D. C. al Coda . . . . repeat from the beginning to ⊕, then skip to Coda.

D. C. al Fine . . . . . repeat from the beginning to the word "Fine."

Decrescendo (>) . gradually softer.

Diminuendo (>) . . gradually softer.

Fermata (⌒) . . . . . hold the note under the sign longer than its full value.

Fine . . . . the end.

First ending (⌐1.⌐) play first time only.

Flat sign (♭) . . . . . lowers a note one half step; play the next key to the left, whether black or white.

Forte (ƒ) . . . . . . loud.

Grand staff. . . . . . the bass staff and the treble staff joined together by a brace.

Half step. . . . . . . the distance from any key to the very next key above or below it (black or white—there is no key between).

Harmonic intervals . distances between notes or keys that are played together.

Incomplete measure a measure at the beginning of a piece with fewer counts than indicated in the time signature. The missing beats are usually found in the last measure.

Intervals . . . . distances between notes or keys.

Key signature . . . . the number of sharps or flats in any key, written at the beginning of each line.

Legato . . . . smoothly connected.

Leger line . . . . . . used above or below the staff to extend its range.

Melodic intervals . . distance between notes or keys that are played separately.

Mezzo forte (mf) . . . moderately loud.

Mezzo piano (mp) . . moderately soft.

Moderato . . . . . . moderately.

Molto . . . . much.

Moto . . . . motion.

Natural sign (♮) . . . cancels a sharp or flat.

Octave . . . . the distance from one key on the keyboard to the next key (lower or higher) with the same letter name.

Octave sign (8va) . . play eight scale tones (one octave) higher when the sign is above the notes; eight scale tones lower when the sign is below the notes.

Pedal mark (⌐___⌐) . press the damper, hold it, and release it.

Phrase . . . . musical thought or sentence.

Pianissimo (pp) . . . very soft.

Piano (p) . . . . soft.

Poco . . . . little.

Poco moto . . . . . . a little motion.

Repeat sign (:‖) . . . repeat from the beginning, or from the first repeat (‖:).

Rests . . . . signs for silence.

Ritardando (rit. or ritard.) . . . . . gradually slowing.

Second ending (⌐2.⌐) play second time only.

Sharp sign (♯) . . . . raises a note one half step; play the next key to the right, whether black or white.

Simile . . . . continue in the same manner.

Slur. . . . . curved line over or under notes on different lines or spaces. Slurs mean to play legato.

Staccato . . . . dots over or under notes meaning to play short, detached.

Subito (sub.) . . . . . suddenly.

Tempo . . . . rate of speed.

Ternary form (ABA) . a piece divided into three sections: A, B, A.

Tetrachord . . . . . . a series of four notes having a pattern of whole step, whole step, half step.

Tied notes . . . . . . notes on the same line or space joined by a curved line and held for the combined values of both notes.

Time signatures . . numbers found at the beginning of a piece or section of a piece. The top number shows the number of beats in each measure. The bottom number shows the kind of note that gets one beat.

Transpose . . . . . . perform in a key other than the original. Each pitch must be raised or lowered by precisely the same interval, which results in the change of key.

Triad . . . . three-note chord.

Vivace . . . . lively.

Whole step . . . . . equal to two half steps; skip one key (black or white).

Appendix C

Appendix C (continued)

Index

Index (continued)